APPLIED LINGUISTICS:

A Survey for Language Teachers

Edited by

Dr. Monika Kehoe
Professor of English,
Chairman, Applied Linguistics,
Marianopolis College, Montreal

Collier-Macmillan International
A Division of The Macmillan Company, New York
Collier-Macmillan Limited, London

Library of Congress Catalogue Card Number: 68-24115

The Macmillan Company, New York
Collier-Macmillan Canada, Limited, Toronto
Collier-Macmillan Limited, London

Printed in the United States of America

PREFACE

This book is written for readers who have no formal training in linguistics but have an interest in language or language teaching. It is meant as a practical text for use in introductory courses in Applied Linguistics. Its emphasis is on second-language teaching.

An effort has been made to bring together in one volume the material, both technical and cultural, essential to an understanding of the field. The compactness of this book is designed to make it useful, especially for summer school and extension teacher-training programs or refresher courses. Because of its wide coverage of the subject and its structured presentation, *Applied Linguistics: A Survey for Language Teachers* may also serve as a handbook for all students seeking concise answers to basic questions about linguistic theory and its practical application.

An attempt has also been made to present the information so that the interested layman may have an overview of the entire field of language and linguistics. It is hoped also that the ambitious teacher will find in these pages the necessary stimulation to further study of some aspect of this fascinating discipline.

The wide coverage and balance of this volume owe much to the contributions of Professors Barkman, Calimag, Elliott, Ellis, and Saint-Pierre. Grateful acknowledgement is also extended to William G. Moulton, Professor of Linguistics in the Department of Germanic Languages at Princeton University, and to the National Education Association for permission to reprint Dr. Moulton's article, "Linguistics." This paper, originally published in the *N.E.A. Journal* (January, 1965), appears here in the Introduction. The professional advice and editorial assistance with the preparation of the manuscript given by Dr. Margaret Gillett, Professor of Education at McGill University, is much appreciated.

Monika Kehoe
Editor

CONTENTS

INTRODUCTION

No subject has received more attention in the sixties than communication. The conquest of space depends upon it. Peace on earth requires it. National survival demands it. Personal success relies on it. Technology is busy with improving communication, and scholarship is dedicated to its exploration. More people are bombarded with more information than ever before and control of the mass media responsible for the barrage becomes a matter of prime political importance.

At the center of this diffusion is the individual, dazed, baffled, not always comprehending the forces shaping his behavior, persuading him to buy this or vote for that. Man, the talking animal, the rational being, is confused, drowning in a deluge of words. His language and his logic are becoming increasingly inadequate to cope with his linguistic environment. Educated in a pre-Telstar era, he finds himself poorly equipped to deal with the new data processing which engulfs him and threatens to make him a social security number with a thumb print.

The next generation, now in the schools, may have a better chance to "get with it," as they say, and exercise some control over the human skid into anonymity. With a better understanding of verbal behavior, the adults of tomorrow will be able to build what Marshall McLuhan calls "defense against media fallout." Their teachers, trained in modern linguistics, will bring a more scientific approach to the entire subject of language, communication, and culture.

LANGUAGE AND CULTURE

In spite of the fact that American linguistics has had a long association with anthropology, the primary focus on language as a tool of culture, rather than as a medium of artistic expression, has not been well understood by many language teachers.

1

With their traditional liberal arts training, "language" and "literature" have been associated in their minds, and the word language has generally meant the written and read form of literature. Likewise "culture" has been interpreted in the nineteenth century sense of refinement as found in belles lettres. Literature rather than language has thus been considered the key to a foreign "culture." For the language teachers who subscribe to this view, the linguist's attack on prescriptive grammar is an abrogation of "correctness" and "values," his concern for the *spoken* language an affront to the appreciation of literature.

But speech is a social instrument, not a status symbol, the linguist claims. He wants to look at what language *is* and does, not what it *ought* to be or do. Its job in the midtwentieth century, he says, is to communicate. The prestige level of communication is something else, the concern of the specialist in sociolinguistics. Social distance measured by dialect peculiarities has its origin in historical patterns which have little relevance to the contemporary world scene. When we divest ourselves of our prejudices and allow ourselves to recognize, for example, that Australian English is not necessarily "bad" English, or Canadian French "bad" French, or Mexican Spanish "bad" Spanish—not bad, but only different, and quite appropriate for communication in Australia or Canada or Mexico—we will not feel apologetic, speaking or teaching any one of them in the area of their currency.

Admittedly, speech may be a social barometer of considerable importance. Its provincial forms, though not inferior in themselves, often label the speaker an "outsider." Language also differentiates one subgroup from another by dialect and even one individual from another by ideolect. What then is "standard" English if it is not the preferred form? What is literature if it is not the record of the culture of a people?

These and many other questions regarding the nature, function and distribution of language, how it is learned and how it is taught most effectively, together with its relation to literature and culture, will be discussed in the following chapters.

THE NATIONAL INTEREST

Much of the impulse given to the scientific study of language by psychologists, sociologists, and others in North America since World War II has come from government money which has financed various programs in language research and the teaching of English overseas. Although no government official would probably be willing to come forward and say so, this generous support is at least a tacit acknowledgment of the importance of language as a political weapon, a device for influencing people, and perhaps, with luck, making a few friends abroad. As further testimony to this awareness, there has also been a greater emphasis than previously on the training of foreign service personnel in the language of the target area of their assignment so that, upon arrival, they can converse fluently in the language of their host country.

Unfortunately, British and American language teachers abroad often share the stigma of "neocolonialism" or "intellectual imperialism" associated with government efforts to expand the use of English. These labels are frequently stamped on such efforts by the more sophisticated members of the ruling classes in the emerging countries of Asia, Africa, the Middle East, and Latin America. Many of the younger generation of "native" government officials in any of the developing areas have themselves been trained in at least one European language which they may come to regard as a threat to their newly articulated national identity. Their distrust is reinforced when they discover, as they sometimes do, the bitter competition, for instance, between British and American attempts to dominate the English language scene.

Still, there is tremendous pressure on the leadership of the developing countries to learn a European language for wider communication. In Africa, either English or French is necessary, in most cases, for the people of one country to communicate with those of another country. Indigenous languages generally do not serve as lingua francas on the "dark continent," (and then only for certain regions as in the case of Swahili in East Africa and Arabic, north of the Sahara). Pan-Africanism requires an international language for its realization, and representatives from all the African states who come to Addis Ababa as delegates to the U.N. Economic Commission for Africa, or the Organization for African Unity must be able to speak either English or French as their working languages. Also, those students who plan to attend universities at home or abroad must, and usually want to, learn a second language for purposes of instruction.

In any event, in most developing countries, the ability to speak a foreign language is limited almost entirely to males and, even then, only to a small proportion of the urban population who have advanced education. Tribal tongues remain the language of home, family, and countryside, if not of national interest. And, as such, they have claim on the emotional life of the individual and are used for all socialization within the various speech communities. European languages are considered necessary political and professional tools and once learned are cherished as status symbols, but they are certainly not thought of by the learners as means to an understanding or appreciation of European culture. In some areas where there is strong anti-white feeling, knowledge of European language may even be disavowed.

Language problems of one kind or another are not restricted to developing countries. For example, the national interest of Belgium, a former imperial power, is involved in the bilingual feud at the University of Louvain. Australia and Canada, ranked internationally among the advanced nations, have large numbers of immigrants who need to learn English (or French, for Quebec) in order to function in the society of their adoption. In Canada, bilingualism is one of the hottest issues on the current political scene. A Royal Commission, set up at Ottawa in July 1963, continues "to inquire into and report upon the existing state of bilingualism and biculturalism in Canada," a situation which the Commissioners themselves describe as "the greatest crisis" in Canadian history. Canadians are aware of the importance of a solution. The preliminary Report of the Commission records that "In all parts of Canada people deplored the lack of qualified staff who could teach the second language competently in the schools"; and notes further that "there was a feeling in many quarters that better techniques for second language teaching are badly needed."

The insights generated by this government-sponsored report may hold true not only for Canada but also for other countries where multilingualism is hampering internal communication and causing disunity. Even so, there are probably some Canadian politicians who would be surprised at the notion that a massive teacher retraining program in second language methodology is called for to rescue the Confederation from threatened dissolution. But the political implications and effects of such a program are clear enough. Most directly it would, if it were linguistically oriented, revolutionize language teaching of both foreign and native tongues. The improved communication and resultant understanding would help to bridge the two cultures that now exist side by side in such splendid isolation.

DEFINITIONS

Communication, we are told, is necessary to establish social ties, to knit people together in reciprocal relationships, to insure human cooperation. *"Social* solidarity is almost synonymous with *linguistic* solidarity."[1] Since communication is fundamental to all aspects of linguistic concern, let us see first in the following section what a distinguished linguist, William Moulton, has to say about this basic process:

How language changes through time, how it varies through space, how it differs from one social group to another, and most of all how it works — these things are studied in linguistics. Because modern linguistics has roots which go back to the early nineteenth century and beyond, many people are familiar with some of the things which interested linguists then and still interest them today.

They find it understandable that a linguist should try to find the line which separates those areas in New England where *barn* is *"barrn"* (with *r*) from those areas where it is *"bahn"* (without *r*); and they may even envy him a bit when he goes to an Indian reservation or South America or Africa to investigate some hitherto undescribed tongue and thus add his little bit to our meager knowledge of the world's 2,000 to 4,000 languages. (No one knows how many there are.)

But when a linguist says that he is doing some research which he hopes will help us understand a little better how it is that "two people are able to talk together," most people shake their heads in puzzlement.

Yet how two people are able to talk together is, of course, the central problem. During the 1930's and 1940's, most American linguists attacked it by trying to work out better techniques of discovering the structure of language — any language — and of analyzing and classifying what they found. Then, in the late 1950's there came a rather dramatic swing in another direction: away from mere classification of data toward a search for universals and a broad, inclusive "theory of language."

In a sense this has been merely a return to some of the prime interests of our nineteenth century predecessors — Wilhelm von Humboldt, for example. It has also brought American linguistics out of the scholarly isolation from which it suffered for a time, and into closer contact with such related disciplines as psychology and philosophy. (The contact with anthropology has always been close.)

How *are* two people able to talk together? Since most of us never ask this question, but take the matter for granted, it is useful to consider just what goes on. Let us assume that we have a speaker A and a hearer B, that A says something to B, and that B understands him without difficulty. Here an act of communication via language has taken place. But *how* did it take place? What went on inside of A? How did the communication move from A to B? And what went on inside of B? The process seems to consist of at least eleven different steps: (See Figure 1-1.)

1) *Semantic encoding.* We assume that A has some sort of "meaning" (or whatever we want to call it) which he wishes to convey to B. His first step is to get this meaning into proper shape for transmission in the language he is using (English, we shall say). Since this is like putting a message in shape to fit the code in which it is to be sent, we can call the process *semantic encoding.*

If A wants to talk to B about some sort of timepiece, his encoding will depend on whether he means the kind that hangs on the wall or stands on a table (a clock), or the kind that is carried in the pocket or worn on the wrist (a watch). In German the single semantic unit *Uhr* includes both types. If he wants to ask whether B "knows" something, he can use the single semantic unit *know.* Spanish would force him to choose between *conocer* (for a person, place, or thing) and *saber* (for a fact).

As these examples show, each language "slices the pie of reality" in its own capricious way. In English, we group a host of different objects, of many types, colors, sizes, and shapes, into the semantic unit *stool.* If to a stool we add a back, however, it suddenly becomes the semantic unit *chair.* If we widen it so that two or more people can sit on it, it is a *bench.* If to a chair we add upholstery, it is still a *chair.* But if to a bench we add upholstery, it suddenly becomes a *sofa.*

Using a bold and imprecise metaphor, we can think of every language as a vast sieve with thousands of semantic slots in it. Any idea which we want to express in that language first has to be put through this sieve. And every language has a special sieve of its own. The dis-

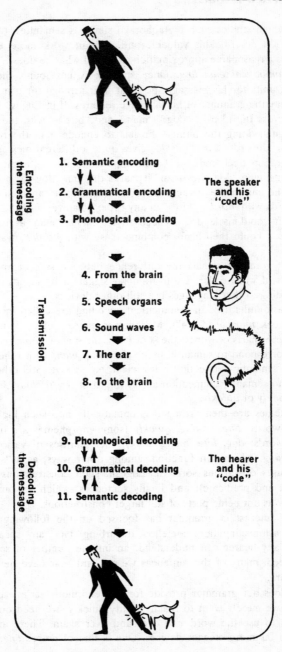

1. **Semantic encoding**
2. **Grammatical encoding**
3. **Phonological encoding**

Encoding the message

The speaker and his "code"

4. **From the brain**
5. **Speech organs**
6. **Sound waves**
7. **The ear**
8. **To the brain**

Transmission

9. **Phonological decoding**
10. **Grammatical decoding**
11. **Semantic decoding**

Decoding the message

The hearer and his "code"

Figure   1-1

cipline which studies such metaphorical sieves is semantics. (A semanticist would describe his valuable and difficult work more elegantly, but this is a reasonable approximation to part of what he does.)

2) *Grammatical encoding.* Once speaker A has found the proper semantic units for his message, he must next arrange them in the particular way the grammar of his language requires. If in English he wants to get across the idea of "dog," "man," and "bite" — with the dog and not the man doing the biting — he has to encode it in the order *dog bites man;* the order *man bites dog* gives quite a different message.

The grammatical code of Latin employs totally different devices. For the meaning "dog bites man" it marks the unit "dog" as nominative (*canis*), the unit "man" as accusative (*virum*), and it can then combine these words with *mordet* "bites" in any order whatever. For the opposite message it would mark "dog" as accusative (*canem*), "man" as nominative (*vir*), and it could then again combine these with *mordet* in any order at all.

English grammar signals the difference between subject and object by means of word order; Latin grammar signals it by means of inflectional endings; other languages use still other devices.

The basic units used in grammatical encoding are called morphemes (from Greek *morphē* "form"). Morphemes may be either words: *dog, bite, man,* or parts of words: the *-s* of *bites,* the *-ing* of *biting,* etc. Some clearly correspond to semantic units; *dog, bite, man;* with others, however, the semantic connection is less clear, e.g. *-s, -ing.* Still others seem to have no semantic connection at all, the *to* of *try to come,* for example, or the *-ly* of *quickly.*

Morphemes are then arranged grammatically into such higher level units as words: *bites, biting, quickly* (some morphemes are of course already words: *dog, bite, man, quick*); then phrases of various sorts, e.g. *the dog* (which can function, among other ways, as a "subject"); then clauses of various sorts (in English, such constructions contain a subject and predicate); and finally sentences, which are marked in some way as not being parts of still larger constructions.

Recent interest in grammar has focused on the following familiar and yet astonishing (and somehow disturbing) fact: any speaker can say, and any hearer can understand, an infinite number of sentences; and, indeed, many of the sentences we say and hear have never been said before.

How does our grammar provide for this enormous variety and flexibility? If we merely want to reach infinity quickly, we need only allow ourselves to use the word *and* over and over again. There are, however, two far more elegant devices. One is that of *embedding:* putting a construction inside a construction inside a construction, etc., like a Chinese puzzle. A classic example is the old nursery tale: "This is the cat that killed the rat that ate the malt (and so on and on and on) . . . that lay in the house that Jack built."

Still more elegant is *transformation,* whereby a basic sentence type may be transformed into a large variety of derived constructions. Thus *the dog bites the man* can be transformed into: *the dog bit (has bitten, had bitten, is biting, was biting, has been biting, can bite, etc.) the man; the man is bitten (was bitten, has been bitten, etc.) by the dog; (the dog) that bites* (etc.) *the man; (the man) that the dog bites; (the man) that is bitten by the dog; (the dog) that the man is bitten by;* etc.

3) *Phonological encoding.* When grammatical encoding has been completed, the message enters the phonological component of the code as a string of morphemes, and these must now be encoded for sound. This is accomplished by encoding each morpheme into one or more basic phonological units or phonemes (from Greek *phōnē* "sound"). The morpheme -*s* of *bites* is converted to the phoneme /s/, *check* to /ček/, *stone* to /stōn/, *thrift* to /θrift/, etc.

(Written symbols for phonemes are customarily placed between slant lines to distinguish them from the letters of regular spelling and from the symbols used in phonetic transcription. Just what symbols are used for phonemes is unimportant; one must merely have a different symbol for each phoneme in the language).

This device of encoding morphemes into *one or more* phonemes each is an extraordinarily powerful one, and in terms of sheer economy it is hard to overestimate its importance. If a language used only one phoneme per morpheme, it could have only as many morphemes as it has phonemes. But if a language uses from one to five phonemes per morpheme (as in the above English examples), the number of possible morpheme shapes soon becomes astronomical.

For a stock of twenty phonemes the figure is 3,368,420; for thirty phonemes it is 25,137,930; and for forty phonemes (English has between thirty and forty, depending on just how you figure them), it reaches the fantastic total of 105,025,640 possible morpheme shapes.

We have given these figures to show what an enormous economy is achieved by having in human language this "duality principle," as it has been called: first an encoding into morphemes, and then a separate encoding of morphemes into one or more phonemes each.

There is, however, a very bad flaw in our figures: We have assumed that it is possible for phonemes to occur in any mathematically possible sequence, such as (for English) /ppppp/, /fstgk/, etc. But English of course does not do this; like every language, it places very strict limitations on possible sequences of phonemes. Nevertheless, even with the strictest sorts of limits, the duality principle permits every language to form far more morpheme shapes than it will ever use.

If we take English to be a thirty-phoneme language (it has more than thirty, no matter how you figure them), permit no morpheme shape or more than five phonemes *(glimpse* /glimps/ actually has six), and assume that only one out of every 1,000 possible sequences can be used, we still end up with a total of 25,137 possible morpheme shapes (the above 25,137,930 divided by 1,000) — enough to take care of any language.

If we remind ourselves that English words can easily consist of three or more morphemes (e.g. *un-friend-li-ness*), it is clear that we are also provided with an overabundance of possible word shapes — more than enough for Lewis Carroll to invent "slithy toves did gyre and gimble in the wabe," using a few of the thousands of available word shapes which had not previously been claimed.

In the preceding paragraphs we have assumed, for purposes of presentation, that a message is neatly encoded first semantically, then grammatically, and then phonologically. But since normal speech is full of false starts, hesitations, grammatical slips, and the like, it seems clear that we behave a good deal more like the young lady who, when told that she should "think before she spoke," replied with rare honesty: "But I can't do that! How do I know what I'm going to say until I start talking?"

If we do not normally plan out our entire message before we start sending it, then we must possess some sort of feedback device which permits us to "monitor" the message as it is sent and to make necessary adjustments as we proceed — adjusting a present tense verb to agree with its singular subject, for example.

4) *From brain to speech organs.* When phonological encoding has been completed, the message has been changed from a string of morphemes to a string of phonemes. Speaker A must now somehow program and send on down to his speech organs a set of instructions telling them what movements to make so as to turn each phoneme into sound. We can compare this with the way paper tapes are punched to provide instructions to automatic typewriters, telegraph transmitters, computers, and the like. Programmed in this way, the message is sent sequentially from the brain to the speech organs.

5) *Movements of the speech organs.* Triggered by successive innervations, the speech organs (vocal cords, tongue, lips, etc.) now perform the proper series of movements. As they do so, an interesting and rather disturbing thing happens. We have assumed that, when the message is sent to the speech organs, it is transmitted in the form of a string of separate instructions, one for each phoneme.

If the message is the word *pin* /pin/, for example, there are first instructions for producing a /p/, then for producing an /i/, and then for producing an /n/. This seems, at least, to be the most reasonable assumption. If the speech organs responded ideally to these instructions, they would first assume the position for /p/, then move jerkily and instantaneously to the position for /i/, then jerkily and instantaneously to the position for /n/.

Common sense tells us that they cannot do this, and X-ray moving pictures of the speech organs in action prove it beyond a doubt. Instead of moving instantaneously from one position to the next, the speech organs bobble back and forth in a constant flow of motion which does not seem to consist of any specific number of segments at all.

A remarkable transformation has taken place. Where the message previously consisted of a string of discrete segments — three, we assume, in the case of /pin/ — it has now been "smeared" into a continuum. As the speech organs move into position to produce the /p/, they already anticipate part of the position for the following /i/. (The reader can test this by whispering the *p*'s of *peer, par, poor*; the sound of each *p* shows clearly which vowel would follow if he went on with the rest of the word.)

As the speech organs then move into the /i/ they carry over part of the position of the /p/ and anticipate part of the position for the following /n/. (We normally "nasalize" such a vowel slightly.) And when the speech organs get to the /n/, they still have part of the position of the proceeding /i/. This drastic change in the shape of the message may seem quite harmless now, but it means that later on this "smeared continuum" of sound will have to be turned back into a string of discrete segments if the message is to be recovered. This is what must take place at stage 9, "phonological decoding."

When the speech organs interact so as to produce a speech sound, they are said to articulate the sound. The study of this aspect of the speech event, *articulatory phonetics,* has long been a highly developed research field.

6) *Vibrations of the air molecules.* As the speech organs articulate, they set the air molecules into vibration and produce audible sound. The study of this aspect of the speech event is *acoustic phonetics.* Here again a great deal of research has been done, and some remarkable advances have been achieved, especially since Word War II.

7) *Vibrations of the ear.* When the vibrations of the air molecules reach hearer B's eardrum, they produce corresponding vibrations which are then transmitted via the three bones of the middle ear to the cochlear fluid of the inner ear. The study of this aspect of the speech event is *auditory phonetics.* It is usually combined with study of the ear in

general, and with the study of auditory perception (which of course involves also the activity of the brain farther up the line).

8) *From ear to brain.* Though this stage is in a sense the mirror image of stage 4, "From brain to speech organs," there are two important differences.

First, when the message went from A's brain to his speech organs, it was transmitted as a string of discrete segments; but since it was then turned into a "smeared continuum" by A's speech organs, this is the shape in which it now reaches B's brain.

Second, speaker A was able to send the message only because, somewhere inside his head, he possessed the proper code; hearer B, however, can receive all the energy in the message whether he knows the code or not — though of course he can do nothing further with it unless he *does* know the same code. We can "hear" all there is to hear in a foreign language message; we can "understand" the message only if we also know the foreign language code.

9, 10, 11) *Phonological, grammatical, and semantic decoding.* Though we surely use these three different types of decoding when we hear and understand a message, the evidence suggests that we do not use them in a step-by-step procedure but rather race back and forth from one to the other, picking up all the information we can get.

Suppose, for example, that we receive a message which we tentatively decode phonologically as, "I hope this'll suture plans." But a second check in the grammatical component now reveals that the phoneme sequence "suture plans" can be grammatically either one of two different things: *suture plans* or *suit your plans.* So we check this *second* possibility in the semantic component of the code. This now "makes sense" — and we accept it.

Our brain can function so swiftly that all of this happens in a flash. Only rarely does this "searching process" take so long that it interferes with our understanding of the speaker's next sentence.

In addition to the message itself, our decoding brings us information of three other types. First, there is information about the identity of the speaker (the quality of his voice tells us that it is Jones and not Smith who is speaking), his state of health (hoarse voice, stuffed up nose), and the like. Such things are presumably the same in all languages and hence not part of any code.

Second, there is the kind of information we often refer to as "it wasn't what he said but how he said it" — things indicating that the speaker is angry, excited, sarcastic, unctuous, etc. Since such matters are different in English from what they are in French or Vietnamese, they are clearly part of the English language in the wider sense of the term. (They also make a fascinating subject for linguistic study.)

Third, there is information as to where the speaker comes from and what social and educational class he belongs to. If he uses the phonological encoding "thoity-thoid," this will suggest that he comes from Brooklyn or thereabouts, if he says "thihty-thihd" we may suspect that he comes from the vicinity of Boston.

If he uses the grammatical encoding "I seen him when he done it," we will place him at a relatively low social and educational level — even though (and this is an interesting point) the message comes through just as clearly as if he had said "I saw him when he did it." Matters of this third sort are also part of the English language in the wider sense of the term.

In the preceding description of a speech event, the part which is of most fundamental interest to the linguist is of course the code itself: its phonological component (here great progress was made in the 1930's and 1940's), its grammatical component (again great progress at that time, and a whole new approach opening up since the late 1950's), and its semantic component (long neglected by American linguists, though there has been a recent revival of interest).

In the preceding paragraphs we have tried to describe a typical speech event, especially that part which is of greatest interest to the linguist: the code itself, the language. When we now look back on what we have found, we are perhaps inclined to say: What is the good of it all? Is it just a game? To the linguist it is far more than a game: it is a thing of beauty and wonder, and it needs no more justification than this. At the same time, with a bit of a sigh, he will admit that it *can* be of practical value. It has obvious applications to foreign language teaching, probably also to the teaching of reading and writing and to English language instruction at all levels. Tentative applications of this sort have already been made; with cooperation on all sides, perhaps they can lead to truly useful results.[2]

LINGUISTIC TERMINOLOGY

As we have seen from Dr. Moulton's essay, linguistics brings a new dimension to language learning and teaching, it introduces a new terminology. Familiar phrases take on different meanings as "language arts" becomes "linguistic science." This alteration does not mean that we are to abandon all efforts at improving the artful use of language by the young. It only means that *our* task as teachers will be made easier and *their* improvement as learners, of their mother tongue or a second language, will be accelerated by *our* understanding of what language is, what it does and how it does it. In order to avoid confusion, let us look now at the basic terms - language, linguist, linguistics, grammar, and applied linguistics - as we shall encounter them in our study.

LANGUAGE

An arbitrary and conventional system of auditory symbols used for social interaction among human beings. In this definition, the word "arbitrary" refers to the capricious choice of sounds which convey meanings, and the absence of logic in their formulation. "Conventional" indicates that the system is learned by all members of any speech community who understand the agreed on meanings. "System" refers to the encoding and decoding process which requires matching before satisfactory communication results between the speaker and the hearer.

The "symbols" involved (not just *signals*) are "auditory" because language is speech (articulate *sound* patterns); the written (graphic) form is derived and therefore not basic to language study as a science. Finally, the function of language is communication, for purposes of "social interaction," while the symbolic nature of language makes it the exclusive prerogative of human beings (Animals use signalling systems but not language). Briefly, then, these are the main elements necessary to a definition of language from the viewpoint of a modern linguist.

LINGUIST

This term has undergone considerable change in the last five centuries. The Oxford dictionary gives the date of its earliest known occurrence as 1588. The common usage, to mean polyglot, or a person "skilled in other tongues besides his own," is the first definition given. The second, "a student of language; a philologist," is dated 1817. In this text "linguist" refers to a trained student of language science (i.e., linguistics) who studies the spoken form of the language and generally knows more than one language well, especially their structures. However, the scientific linguist is not necessarily fluent in more than one language.

What does a scientific linguist do? This depends largely on the kind and amount of training he has had. First of all, in an academic setting, the person with a Ph.D. in Linguistics may do research, either in an exotic language or in any aspect of the better known languages, not yet investigated. If he has been trained at an American university, his approach is usually descriptive (see below). He may, of course, teach some phase of the subject at the university level. (There is an increasing demand for such specialists at Canadian universities.) With an M.A., one may teach his mother tongue as a second language, either at the secondary or college level, or supervise programs of second language teaching in the lower schools, including those arranged for adults. The Ed.D., awarded for specialization in Applied Linguistics, (see below) particularly qualifies the person holding it for training language teachers in Schools or Faculties of Education. [3]

LINGUISTICS

First of all there is the historical or "diachronic" study of languages. This approach, related to philology, is concerned with (1) language classification, (2) methods of collecting data on language, (3) analysis of this material, (4) language change, (5) comparative study of languages in their written forms, (6) additional matters such as translation, stylistics, and normative or prescriptive (traditional) grammar. The diachronic approach was characteristic of language study before the twentieth century and continues as a major interest particularly of European linguists. It has two aspects: (a) the development of a language through its history or *linguistic phylogeny,* and (b) the study of the development of speech habits in children or *linguistic ontogeny.* The latter is now carried on as a phase of psycholinguistics. It may, therefore, be thought of as a link between the diachronic and the synchronic approaches.

Secondly, there is the descriptive or "synchronic" study of languages. This approach is related to the behavioral sciences and, in America, has evolved from field work in cultural anthropology. It is concerned with analysis and observation of *spoken* languages, particularly their structure, hence it has also been called "structural linguistics." Descriptive structural linguistics has been developed mainly in the U.S.A. after 1850. Since descriptive linguistics is usually divided into three major sections: (1) phonemics, (2) morphemics, and (3) syntax, some explanation of these terms is necessary to an understanding of the new "grammar".

Phonemics (Phonology)

The systematic study of the class of sounds which alter meaning and distinguish words in a language; the function of these sounds. Two kinds of phonemes are recognized: (a) segmental phonemes, or those units of sound which, strung together, make up a word, and (b) suprasegmental phonemes, or the intensity, pitch, stress and juncture of the sounds of any utterance. (These categories are also applied to morphemes by some linguists.) Descriptive linguistics uses *phonetics* to record the sounds of human speech. Phonetics has two subdivisions: (a) articulatory and auditory phonetics, related to physiology, and concerned with the production and perception of speech sounds, and (b) acoustic phonetics, a branch of physics, which describes the physical features of the sounds.

Morphemics (Morphology)

The systematic study of the units of sound which carry meaning in a language; the structure of words.

Syntax

That part of the grammar of a language which deals with the structure of the sentence and the arrangement of the words therein.

GRAMMAR

The analysis of the structure of a language; a device for generating the sentences of a language. In the midtwentieth century, the term grammar covers a complex of concepts difficult to disentangle. In general, there has been a shift from the traditional (classical, Latinate, prescriptive, normative, rules-conscious, authoritative), "correct" formula of the nineteenth century to the "modern" (structural, functional, transformational, generative), linguistic approach of the present century. The focus of attention has moved, too, from the analysis of parts of speech to the construction of the sentence and from the examination of written languages to the description of spoken tongues.

APPLIED LINGUISTICS

The theory of linguistics put into practice in these various fields:

1) Geography — in the preparation of linguistic atlases and maps defining dialect areas.

2) Lexicography — in the making of dictionaries (e.g. the Oxford English Dictionary and Webster's controversial *Third International*).

3) Medicine — in the developing of orthopsychiatric and psychotherapeutic techniques; in the treatment of speech pathologies, aphasic and other verbally related disorders.

4) Engineering — in architectural design involving acoustics; in cybernetics.

5) Pedagogy — in the teaching of languages, both the mother tongue and foreign languages; in the appreciation of literature.

The applied linguist as a pedagogue, studies the structural rationale of a language and applies it to the teaching situation with one or the other of the following approaches: (a) structural or (b) transformational. (For explanation, see Chapter II)

The present survey focuses on the application of linguistics to pedagogy, particularly to the teaching of English as a second language. It relies on various authorities in the field who may be associated with "schools" of linguistics.

SCHOOLS OF LINGUISTICS[4]

THE EUROPEAN OR CONTINENTAL SCHOOL

With its scholarly roots in comparative philology, this school is generally more theoretical and philosophical in its approach than the British or American. The European writer on language whose name is probably best known outside of Europe is Otto Jespersen (1860-1943), the Danish philologist. His contribution to phonetics and his monumental *A Modern English Grammar on Historical Principles* (7 vols, 1909-1949) brought current knowledge of linguistics to bear upon the fields of phonology and grammar.

One of the early workers in the science of meaning, another favorite area of inquiry on the Continent, was the distinguished French scholar Michel Bréal, who has been credited with coining the word "semantics" which he used as the title of his book, *Essai de Sémantique* (1897, subtitled in the English edition of 1910, "Studies in the Science of Meaning.") The most important figure in the European tradition was undoubtedly Ferdinand de Saussure (1857-1913), an eminent Swiss comparativist and theoretician, whose work (not published until after death) was widely influential in Europe and on the development of American descriptive/structural linguistics.

In the realm of pure theory, the "glossematics" of the Copenhagen group, as set forth in Louis Hjelmslev's *Prolegomena* to a *Theory of Language* (English translation, 1953) represents one of the most abstract approaches developed so far from de Saussure's theses. Still in its infancy, glossematics attempts to construct a rigorous system of language analysis which is entirely logical and independent of all nonlinguistic phenomena. It is typical of the extreme refinement of the efforts of the Europeans to define a precise formulation of linguistic theory. The persistent interest of the Continental linguists in Indo-European languages and problems of change are reflected in *Les Mutations consonantiques de germanique* (Paris, 1956) by Jean Fourquet, as well as in the research of André Martinet and others at the Sorbonne.

One of the most influential of the early writers of the Prague Circle, another important group of linguistic researchers, was Nikolas S. Trubetzkoy (1890-1938) whose *Principles of Phonology* (Prague, 1939) has been widely studied. Recent members of the Prague Circle seem to prefer to investigate questions of stylistics as they are found in literature, an interest which they have come to share with their British colleagues.[5]

As a result of the World War II, a number of refugees from central Europe congregated in London and New York where they attempted to organize universities in exile. As part of this effort to carry on their work overseas, a few linguists joined with their American counterparts to found the Linguistics Circle of New York which became a meeting ground for European and American viewpoints. Through its journal, *Word,* (founded in 1945) the LCNY has extended its influence far beyond the metropolitan area and one of the outcomes of the resulting interaction has been a tendency toward a mutual accommodation of scholarly approaches.

THE BRITISH SCHOOL

Sometimes referred to as the "Neo-Firthians," this school was firmly established with the appointment of the late J. R. Firth to the first Chair of General Linguistics at the University of London in 1944. The fact that this new position was located in the School of Oriental and African studies gives a clue to the general direction of its intended research, as well as to the particular interests of Professor Firth himself.

Precursors to Firth were Sweet and Palmer, whose influence on the development of applied linguistics has been enormous. The English school of phonetics, launched by H. Sweet with his late nineteenth century *Handbook* on the subject, has expanded to include many other subjects of related interest: linguistic pedagogy, speech defects, orthographies for Oriental and African languages, spelling reform, dialectology, lexicography, to name only a few.

Because of the widespread use of English in Commonwealth countries and British colonial areas throughout the world, linguistic pedagogy has received considerable attention from members of the British group. (For additional details see Chapter V). In Sweet's own time, the Direct Method of teaching English as a foreign language was developed. Indeed, it was Sweet himself who laid down the basic rules: (a) choose one variety of the language, (b) limit the amount taught in any one course, (c) arrange the material in the order of skills to be learned, namely, aural comprehension, speaking, reading, and writing, (d) grade the materials used and present them in a sequence according to difficulty. Sweet, in turn, influenced Harold Palmer whose first important work on method, *The Scientific Study and Teaching of Languages* came out in 1917. These were radical departures from the traditional methodology of the early twentieth century.

Today the centers of linguistic research in England are, of course, the major universities, where various individuals are studying special aspects of the subject. Durham, Essex, Leeds, Liverpool, and London are particularly active at present. Randolph Quirk's projected *Survey of Educated Spoken English,* soon due for completion, is anticipated as a major contribution to descriptive linguistics. The paperback series, *Language and Language Learning,* issued by the Oxford University Press, London, is bringing into wider circulation much of the current linguistic work being done in Britain and the Commonwealth.

THE AMERICAN SCHOOL

This school of linguistics, usually thought of as a newcomer, may be traced back to the writings of William Dwight Whitney of Yale University whose book, *Language and the Study of Language: Twelve Lectures on the Principles of Linguistic Science* (1867), constituted the basis of instruction in the field a century ago. However, it was not until the turn of the century that American linguistics began to take on its special characteristics and its new direction in grammatical studies.

In the Introduction to his *Handbook of American Indian Languages* (1911), Franz Boas, a European-trained anthropologist, teaching at Columbia University, set forth the concept of analytical grammar which gave a new precision to the study of language structure. His more rigorous method was followed by that of his student, Edward Sapir, who insisted on meticulous analysis of the spoken language through the use of native informants. Sapir's investigations, like those of his teacher, were concentrated on American Indian languages and their sound systems. Because of the difficulties in translating these exotic tongues into English, there developed a suspicion of meaning as a basis for analysis and an attempt to substitute structure in its stead. Many American linguistics continue to consider meaning as a somewhat peripheral concern, more properly within the purview of psychology and philosophy (semantics).

Although the anthropological approach was distinctly American in its origin, descriptive linguistics had a parallel development in Europe where the leading figure was the Swiss linguist, Ferdinand de Saussure, mentioned previously. From him, Bloomfield, the great synthesizer, must have absorbed at least some ideas. *Language* (1933), Bloomfield's classic text, a revision of an earlier publication of 1914, reflects many aspects of de Saussure's theories, a possible indication that both men were pursuing similar lines of inquiry at about the same time.[6] At any rate, Bloomfield succeeded in assembling, within the scope of a single volume, all that had been achieved so far in the field, at the same time that he pointed the way for countless subsequent achievements in structural linguistics. The entire shift from item-centered (vocabulary, sentences, meanings, sounds) to structure-centered (patterns) thinking about language stems from suggestions outlined in the work of Bloomfield and his disciples. Much of the investigation done by contemporary American linguists, of whom C. C. Fries is the doyen, explores the patterns of structure and their function as signals in a system.

The application of linguistic theory to pedagogy is an area of concern which American scholars share with their British colleagues. Since World War II, great strides have been made in Applied Linguistics, particularly in the teaching of English as a second language (TESL). Beginning in 1942 with the War Relocation Authority (the Federal agency that evacuated Japanese from the West Coast), the U. S. government has given substantial aid to various TESL projects at home and overseas.[7] Each of the military services developed language training centers for its personnel and an Army Language Method which included "Area Studies" evolved. The Army Language Institute (now the Defense Language Institute) at Monterey, California became famous for the innovations (which included mechanical aids as well as native informants) of its intensive, and, at the time, "radical" approach to the teaching of second languages.

USIS (U. S. Information Service) and AID (Agency for International Development) both conduct extensive TESL operations in developing areas. English specialists are also sent to these countries under individual university contracts, while members of the Peace Corps frequently fill vacancies for English teachers in the secondary schools. (For further details, see Chapter VI).

Since 1958, the U. S. Office of Education (under the National Defense Education Act, Title VI) has supported language study and research, both by individuals and institutions, which called for the expenditure of millions of dollars each year on the teaching and for improvement in the teaching of "critically needed" and "commonly taught" languages. The sudden and significant involvement of the U. S. government in linguistics gave a strong impetus to the field, identifying it as one in which it was possible to have a career other than ordinary classroom teaching. This stimulated linguistic study at the university level and a number of institutes, departments, and graduate programs were inaugurated to deal with the demand. Almost overnight a traditionally monolingual society with little interest in language learning, except as a dilettante pastime, has become one in which commitment to foreign language study is a matter of major national interest. With the maturation of American linguistics, there has come an increasing concern for theory and interdisciplinary contacts outside the field of anthropology. These combined interests which have begun to develop into new branches of study have sometimes resulted from the tenuous position linguistics has held in the past as a "related" academic course, taught in conjunction with other studies of a more traditional (hence acceptable) nature.

LINGUISTICS IN CANADA

This role of "poor relation" persists in Canada where linguistics is only beginning to be fully accepted as a respectable academic discipline in its own right and is still taught, in some universities, in isolated courses or under the aegis of other "established" departments or institutes. In general, research in linguistics done in Canada, at the English-speaking universities, follows the American pattern, with work in Amerindian languages and in dialectology among the main concerns. Research at the Universities of Montreal and Laval, on the other hand, bears a stronger European influence, and more study is, as might be expected, given to French-Canadian subject matter.[8] Some of the projects undertaken at various Canadian Universities include a *Dictionary of Canadianisms*,[9] compiled at the Lexicographical Center of the University of Victoria, and a Summer School of Linguistics on the Edmonton campus of the University of Alberta (where in July 1964 a conference on Indigenous Languages of North America was held). Field work in dialectology is also being pursued at Memorial University, Newfoundland and in British Columbia, while that done in southwest Nova Scotia is awaiting publication. The Canadian Linguistic Association enrolls, among its 400-plus members, most of those involved in research and teaching in the field. All major universities and their affiliated institutions are represented in the organization which publishes its quarterly journal in both French and English.

One of the persisting problems facing applied linguistics in Canada, as previously mentioned, is that of bilingualism which is, of course, inextricably interwoven with biculturalism.[10] In the General Introduction to Book I of its Report (Queen's Printer, Ottawa, October 8, 1967), the "B & B" Commission, as it is popularly known, has defined fully, in the framework of its own reference, the terms of its title. There are more than eleven pages devoted to the meaning of language and culture in the French/English Canadian context and anyone desiring to understand the language problem in Canada will be compelled to study, not only the Introduction, but the entire Report as its ten books (or volumes) are published.

While Canadians look to "B & B" to bridge their two solitudes, the Kremlin and the White House have their "hot line," the U. N. has its simultaneous interpreters, the planet has its intercontinental satellites and all are trying to establish communication across some sort of space-time interval, either physical or psychological, or both. The linguistic phenomena of this attempted exchange are tremendous. The better they are understood, the greater the probability of success for an effort which may be of even more importance to another generation than it has been to ours.

M. K.

---

[1]Joyce O. Hertzler, *A Sociology of Language* (New York: Random House, 1965), p. 65

[2]William G. Moulton, "Linguistics," *NEA Journal,* January 1965; reprinted with the kind permission of the author and the National Education Association.

[3]Other employment opportunities and careers are discussed in Chapter VI.

[4]The following regional breakdown into "schools" is not intended as a definitive analyses of differences among these groups, but only as area profiles for identification and reference purposes.

[5]See Paul L. Garvin, (ed. and trans.), *Prague School Reader on Esthetics, Literary Structure and Style* (Washington D. C.: Georgetown University Press, The Institute of Languages and Linguistics, 1964).

[6]De Saussure's *Cours* was first published in French in 1916 but was not translated into English until 1959.

[7]See M. Kehoe, "The Teaching of English as a Second Language," *Bulletin* of the Institute of Education, McGill University, Macdonald College, Montreal, March 1965, p. 12.

[8]For a list of courses in "Didactics" at Laval University, see Chapter VI.

[9]The *Senior Dictionary of Canadian English* for high schools (Scarborough, Ont.: W. J. Gage, Ltd., 1967) is one of a series produced by Canadian linguists.

[10]The principal authorities on bilingualism are Canadians: W. E. Lambert of McGill University and W. F. Mackey of Université de Laval.

I LANGUAGE LEARNING

Gaston Saint-Pierre

THE NATIVE LANGUAGE AND THE SECOND

In an age when knowledge of foreign languages has become so vitally important in the life of nations and of so many individuals, the most casual observer cannot but wonder whether the limited success achieved in the teaching and learning of foreign languages has really warranted the investment in time, energy, and money. Some forty years or so ago, Bloomfield deplored the sad state of language teaching. It was his belief that teaching language without a knowledge of its nature could only "waste years of every child's life and reach a poor result." Unfortunately, these views are perhaps just as valid today as they were then, and they have been reiterated since in various forms by leading educators.

That the teaching and learning of foreign languages has too generally been wide of the mark is due in part to a misguided notion of speech, its operation, and the language learning process. To be sure, language is a highly complex activity, involving an amazingly large number of mental and motor operations. But the fact that so many human beings achieve a command of their native language early in life may convey the mistaken impression that mastering a language is indeed all too common an achievement to call for any particular skill. Since we have already unconsciously mastered the fundamentals of our native tongue and been through the process of actual language learning by the time we start taking formal language instruction in school, we are unaware of the difficulties involved in the task.

The aural-oral skills needed for fluency of speech in the native language are acquired only after years of constant practice of structural patterns, vocabulary items, and speech sounds. However, when it comes to learning a second language, the problems confronting the adult learner are of a different kind. For one thing, his physiological make-up lacks the plasticity characteristic of infancy. His auditory equipment as well as his articulatory organs are no longer as responsive to language training as they once were. Motor skills involved in speech are less easily developed. And the older the adult learner is, the more obdurate and less responsive these speech mechanisms are to training. Speech habits in the adult are more or less deeply imbedded in his subconscious, and the structure of the native language tends to rebel against the introduction of any linguistic scheme conflicting with the patterns of the vernacular. "The force in the structural arrangements of the first language," writes Fries, "makes the learning of a second language as an adult a very different matter from the learning of the first language." [1]

Since foreign language training generally starts some years after schooling has begun and since class instruction in the native language has been, from the start, mostly if not exclusively focused on writing skills, the foreign language learner has come to think of language primarily as a form of written communication and to relegate to the background its very essence, *oral* communication. This all-too-prevalent misconception is no doubt largely responsible for the undue stress placed on the written word in foreign language instruction, more particularly in the initial stage when attention should be concentrated on developing audio-lingual skills.

In any event, the adult learner is strongly influenced by his earlier academic background, and it is only with the greatest difficulty that he can pry himself away from the habit of equating language with writing. There is the ever-present tendency on his part to look to the written word for an answer to his linguistic difficulties, and unless this tendency is strongly and constantly resisted, foreign language learning is bound to be a frustrating experience. Learning a language consists, as a first step, in learning its phonological system. It is, among other things, and especially with regard to second language learning, a matter of training the ear to perceive the foreign speech sounds, to discriminate among them, and to distinguish them from those of the vernacular. After this has been attended to, then comes the business of forming the foreign sounds by the speech organs.

To try to represent on paper, voice sounds such as are produced in speech can only be subjective and, at best, inadequate. To depend on a written text for learning spoken language is courting trouble. It becomes confusion compounded when, added to the shortcomings of the printed word, a language (such as English or French) uses a form of spelling that is largely inconsistent. One could easily cite from these languages, instances where a speech sound is represented by a variety of letters (graphemes) and conversely where the same graphemes may represent a distinct voice sound.

The written word can also constitute a stumbling block, although of a different kind, for the native speaker first learning his mother tongue. His problem, however, differs from that of the foreign language learner who hopelessly seeks in the written word information to guide him in producing the spoken language. The native speaker must concentrate his efforts on associating symbols with the speech sounds he already knows. Generally, he does not have to cope with the phonetic difficulties that face the foreign language learner. It is only a matter of his learning how the speech sounds of his mother tongue are represented in writing and how to match sets of graphic symbols with the spoken sounds. The pattern followed by a child in the process of learning his native tongue points to the priority of speech over writing in foreign language learning. The adult foreign language learner who, therefore, attempts — futilely — to learn a second language through the medium of the written word, reverses the natural process of language learning and violates the very concept of language.

If, in some respects, foreign language learning seems similar to native language learning, it is, in other respects, quite different. This is particularly so in the case of the foreign language learner who, in his attempt to develop reading skills in the foreign language tries to interpret the written word in terms of his own phonological system. Whatever unit or combination of speech sounds the native speaker tags on to the symbols used to represent the language he speaks, these will be sounds belonging in the phonological system of the language. However, since no two languages have identical phonological structures, it is just about impossible for a foreign language learner, who only has his own phonological system to fall back on, ever to achieve a command of the target language on the strength of the written word only.

It follows from this, that the foreign language learner should become familiar with the speech sounds of the target language *before* he is called upon to interpret its written form. This is not meant to disparage or underestimate the written word, obviously, but rather to underscore the significant distinctions between it and the spoken form and the necessity for resorting to appropriate techniques in dealing with them.

APPROACHES AND TECHNIQUES

Generally, the methods of foreign language teaching that have been resorted to in the past have reflected the conception (or misconception) of language of the day and have often been at variance with one another. Among the kinds of foreign language instruction that have had the widest circulation, perhaps the most notable are the grammar-translation and direct methods. More recent approaches are the audio-lingual and the oral.

THE GRAMMAR-TRANSLATION METHOD

As the name implies, this method is characterized by its insistence upon the rules of grammar based on memory and reasoning. The foreign language learner is expected to acquire by rote paradigms, inflections, or whatever morphological features are distinctive of the target language. The bilingual dictionary and grammar book are important aids in translation. Attention is centered on analysis and parsing. The learner is expected to reason out grammar rules before putting them into application. Training in audio-lingual skills is treated marginally, if at all. Language learning itself is attempted mainly through paper work. If the grammar-translation method were specifically designed to investigate only the material resources of written language, then it might be an acceptable means for achieving its aim. But to depend on this method in the teaching and learning of a foreign language can only spell trouble and lead to frustration. It is a carry-over from the days when the classical ("dead") languages were the staple of education and were studied by the elite for purely academic purposes.

With the advent of linguistics and the gradual realization that language is sound, first and foremost, it became increasingly difficult to formulate an effective pedagogical technique that did not take this new science into consideration. From then on it became self-evident to enlightened language teachers that the traditional grammar-translation method or any other springing from the same view of language would fail.

THE DIRECT METHOD

Dissatisfaction with the translation method and the meager results obtained led eventually to the development of the direct method. Proponents of this method felt that the teaching and learning of foreign languages would achieve better results if they were patterned on the priorities followed in the acquisition of the native tongue. Translation was therefore discarded.

The one identifying feature of the direct method is that language is learned in contact as well as in context; that is, from the earliest stages, the student is led to use the target language as much as possible within meaningful situations. The vocabulary taught refers to objects that are present in the classroom or are part of the student's immediate personal experience. Association of words and sentences with meaning is achieved through dramatization. In fact, the situational element is the very fabric of the direct method.

A number of other methods, bearing different names but built along closely related lines, also use the same approach. The foreign language is, as much as possible, integrated with the student's life. In brief, environmental factors determine in large part the direction of the language learning activity. Use of the vernacular is avoided. A great deal of imagination, resourcefulness, and ingenuity is demanded of the teacher using the direct method, since the instructional material being practiced is largely determined by the context in which the class finds itself. He must, often on the spur of the moment, adjust the dialogue to the situation at hand and maintain as much realism as possible.

THE AUDIO—LINGUAL APPROACH

Unfortunately, the direct method does not take notice of the psycho-linguistic elements in foreign language learning and consequently fails to provide for the adult learner's disadvantages. In its approach to foreign language teaching, the audio-lingual method comes one step closer to reality in the scientific application of modern linguistic concepts. At the early stages of the student's training, the audio-lingual method insists upon developing auditory perception, discrimination, and speech skills. It is similar to the direct method in this respect. The material of instruction is selected and designed with those ends in view. Basic sentence patterns are memorized and reading and writing are put off until the learner has acquired a reasonable aural-oral command of the fundamental structures (phonological, morphological, and syntactic) of the target language. As might be expected from its very name, use of translation as a learning device is rejected entirely.

What may be said to differentiate the audio-lingual method from the direct is that, in the former, the emphasis lies, above all, on sharpening the ear to foreign speech sounds, on training the vocal organs to produce such sounds and on developing speech automatisms necessary for spontaneity of expression. In the case of the direct method, instruction is mainly context oriented and made to represent, as much as is possible in the classroom environment, actual or real situations. The motor activities of language, which receive particular attention in the audio-lingual method, are treated incidentally in the direct method. Classroom activity revolves around the personal experience of the student.

THE ORAL APPROACH

This approach, which has come to the fore in recent years, differs markedly from either the direct method or the audio-lingual approaches. Fries, a pioneer in its diffusion, claims "The oral approach is primarily a name to describe the end to be attained in the first stage of language learning rather than a descriptive limitation of the permissible devices to attain that end." [2]

As implied, the oral approach is concerned with linguistic rather than pedagogical factors in foreign language learning. According to its principles, the oral approach, while being essentially audio-lingual, does not necessarily reject reading and writing *a priori,* if they can be of any help in the acquisition of foreign languages. But in actual practice, these skills come into their own *after* the first stage of learning, when time and effort have been devoted to mastering the basic structural patterns with only a limited vocabulary. The aim of the oral approach is to train the learner to "produce [the required response] orally, automatically, and without hesitation" in the presence of appropriate stimulus.

In fact, the oral approach is not in itself a teaching technique or a method, but an objective to be attained, i.e., the ability to use the target language at normal speed and with freedom, with native, or near-native, ease. Furthermore, the assumption that foreign language teaching, in order to be effective, must rest as much upon an analysis of the source language as the target language is a corollary of the oral approach. Basically, the purpose of an analysis of this sort is to isolate the contrastive elements of the two language systems and to exploit their differences in the preparation of instructional materials. Points of contrasts serve as guidelines in the choice of exercises and pattern practices. In this linguistic approach, oral features such as intonation, stress, pitch, and structural signals generally come under close scrutiny. Rules of grammar are learned incidentally as a result of intensive pattern practice, first in meaningful situations and then in reinforcement exercises.

Of the several foreign language techniques described above, the oral approach is clearly the one which gets at the root of the matter. It grapples directly with the fundamental teaching and learning problems. It is also the one that imposes the greatest demands upon the teacher and textbook writer, since it presupposes a solid knowledge of and deep insight into the working of language.

To sum up: The translation-method failed mainly because it was based on the false assumption that the written form of language was the most important and it ignored the essentially oral features of speech. It extended to foreign languages the same treatment it did to classical languages, regarding them as tongues no longer spoken, but studied for whatever "cultural values" could be derived from scrutinizing the written word. It transferred to the study of modern foreign languages time-honored practices that violated basic principles of learning and linguistics, such as subjecting the student to memorizing endless lists of paradigms, declensions, and other linguistic forms.

As for the direct method, it failed to take into account the fact that the linguistic needs of the adult learner are not necessarily the same as those of the child. The conditions under which foreign language training is conducted in adult life are different from those prevailing in childhood. In his early years, the child has no alternative but to learn his maternal tongue unconsciously, in a somewhat haphazard manner, by trial and error. The linguistic adult can ill-afford to follow such an uneconomical course of action.

The techniques of the audio-lingual method, by stressing activities designed to develop auditory perception and oral production in an orderly fashion, aim more directly at overcoming some of the basic problems of foreign language learning. The oral approach has, in addition, the merit of putting emphasis on the points of contrasts between the native and the target language and directing attention to the need for carefully graded materials of instruction.

CONTRASTIVE ANALYSIS

A cursory review of a few linguistic difficulties likely to interfere with the learning of English by a French speaker will serve to illustrate how descriptive linguistics and, more specifically, contrastive analysis operate in facilitating foreign language learning by the oral approach.

Starting at the phonological level, we are all aware that the speech sounds — known technically as phonemes — of one language are different from those of another. The fact that the phonemes of a language are sometimes said to sound "strange" to a nonspeaker of that language is evidence that these phonemes do not belong in the phonological system of the person attempting to reproduce them. To take French, for instance, the vowel *i*, in *habit* (the final *t* is here silent) is different from the *i* sound in English *bee*. A discriminating ear would possibly detect this phonetic difference, which, by the way, is generally not perceived by the average person. Another difference is the opposition between [ɪ], as in *ship*, and [i], as in *sheep*, in English. In French, a vowel sound approximating English [ɪ] is sometimes substituted for [i] in certain phonetic contexts, while still belonging in the [i] class of speech sounds. In the French words *ri* (laughed) and *ride* (wrinkle), the *i's*, although phonetically dissimilar, are still of the same kind. Not so in English. Apart from the fact that these phonemes are different in various respects from one language to another, they are moreover *significantly* different from each other in English, in so far as the substitution of one for the other changes the meaning of the word. Compare *rid* [rɪd] and *reed* [rid].

There are cases also where one language may have in its phonological system a phoneme, and in most cases it has several, which not only differs in a minor way from its counterpart in another system, but which is altogether absent from the other system. French [p] and English [p] are slightly different, but [θ], as in *think* (th), and [ð], as in *then* (th), are totally absent from French, which has no such phonemes at all. A thorough contrastive analysis of the phonological systems of French and English would bring out the phonetic oppositions between these two languages and thus serve to predict the linguistic interferences which the French speaker is bound to meet in trying to speak English. It is imperative that instructional material pays special attention to these areas of conflict. But before the foreign language learner attempts to practice the phonemes of the language under study, it is essential for the teacher to ensure that, first of all, the ear of the student has been trained not only to discriminate the foreign phonemes from those of the vernacular, but also to distinguish between the phonemes in the target language. It is only after this has been accomplished that the learner is in a position to achieve a satisfactory pronunciation of the foreign tongue.

It might perhaps be appropriate to point out in this connection that it is not enough for the foreign language learner to know how to pronounce the foreign phonemes singly. Since these are hardly ever used in isolation, it is important that he should be trained to link them up properly in speech, a process known as "catenation" and one which is essential for naturalness of expression.

PHONOLOGICAL LEVEL

There are obviously other areas of language which should come under close scrutiny, not only in the teaching of English to French speakers, but also in the teaching and learning of foreign languages generally. One such area is that covered by suprasegmental phonemes, such as intonation and stress, as opposed to segmental phonemes, the vowels and consonants of language. A scientific analysis of the intonation patterns of these two languages would soon point to basic differences. In fact, any speaker who has had the experience of hearing his native tongue spoken by foreigners could not have failed to observe how often they carry over into his mother tongue the melody or intonation contours of their own vernaculars. The melody of a language is just as much part and parcel of speech as are other linguistic features. Intonation can be of vital importance in communication. For instance, using a falling intonation in an utterance such as the following: *He is,* conveys, short as it is, a radically different message from the same utterance ending with a rising intonation: *He is?* In the first case, the utterance is obviously a statement, whereas, in the second, it is a question. Such patterns as these would not pose a problem for a French learner of English, since they run parallel to those in his own native tongue, but this is far from always the case. Conflicts in intonation patterns between these two languages are perhaps more readily observable in longer utterances than in the shorter ones presented above.

Another suprasegmental phoneme of prime importance in some languages (and English is one of them while French is not) is *stress,* more specifically, syllable stress. As the name implies, it is a linguistic feature according to which certain syllables receive greater prominence than others. Nominally, French has one syllable stress which falls on the last syllable of words. In actual practice however, such stress is generally ignored in conversational speech, contrary to English where stress is just as much part of words as are segmental phonemes. In fact, every word in English has at least one primary stress, which in polysyllabic words may affect one syllable or another. Furthermore, the misplacing of the stress in English may occasion a change in meaning. Such is the case with regard to the word *súrvey* which, as a noun, is generally stressed on the first syllable. As a verb, *survéy* is stressed on the second syllable. So also with the verb *permít* as opposed to the noun *pérmit*. These and other linguistic peculiarities of English have, in the course of years of speaking, become so much a part of the mental make-up of the native speaker that he takes them for granted. Yet, the fact that almost any misstressed word he hears causes him to be perplexed is evidence that syllable stressing is a relevant characteristic of English speech. It may be added also that any omission of this linguistic feature would make English seem unnatural at best. One may then easily imagine the linguistic difficulties confronting the French learner of English who, as the speaker of an unstressed language, except in case of emotion or emphasis, is confronted with a language system in which word stress is one of its fundamental characteristics. Emotional or emphatic stress can also constitute a problem for the French learner of English. The utterance *He did it*, with a strong emphatic stress on *He*, has to be rendered quite differently in French, to wit, *C'est lui qui l'a fait*. The French system of stress has no parallel form for expressing emphasis of this kind.

It is indeed of little help for the learner to know that aside from a few general rules of limited application, word stress in English assumes no clear pattern. "Generally speaking," says Jones in his classic work, *An Outline of English Phonetics*, "there are no rules determining which syllable or syllables of polysyllabic English words bear the main stress. The foreign student is obliged to learn the stress of each word individually."[3] Again this is cold comfort for the learner seeking assistance or a practical course of action for making the right use of stress in English. A French speaker learning word stress in English may have a difficulty similar to that of an English speaker learning gender in French. Every vernacular has its own set of potential language problems for the foreign language learner, and these problems are mainly traceable to the structural features of the native language and the speech habits of the learner.

An examination therefore of the phonetic features of both the source language and the target language would bring to light whatever phonological discrepancies exist between the two systems. Such contrastive analysis warns both the foreign language teacher and learner of the linguistic traps in their path, in the same way as other levels of analysis do with respect to other areas of language. Linguistic analysis can also help immeasurably, through a selection of appropriate instructional material, in calling the attention of the learner, not only to the presence of syllabic stress in English — and this is of particular import if his native tongue shares no such phonological characteristic — but also to the interaction of the stressed syllable upon the adjacent vowels. If he is made to realize that, in English, vowels coming next to a stressed syllable, whether preceding or following it, are very often obscured; if he is made to observe how, as in his own vernacular, segmental phonemes used in sequences, such as they are in words, affect one another in phonetic ways that are typical of each language; and, most important of all, if he is given instruction designed to develop the habit of stressing words in English, the result is bound to be rewarding.

MORPHOLOGICAL LEVEL

A similar use of contrastive linguistics can be resorted to at the morphological level in order to make foreign language learning more profitable. To adduce an example from French -English again: *Signalling of plural* is expressed quite differently in spoken French and in spoken English. In the words *books, pencils* and *classes*, the more-than-one notion is expressed in English by means of the ending, viz. [-s] (book*s*), [-z] (pencil*s*), and [-əz] (class*es*). In French, however, the same plural concept is signalled before the word and through the article (as far as words beginning with a consonant are concerned). Example lə livr (*le livre* - the book), le livr (*les livres* - the books).

Since nouns are nearly always preceded by an article in French, it follows from the above that in the teaching and learning of

French as a foreign language, the article is best treated as a type of prefix announcing either the singular or the plural, as well as the masculine or the feminine. Considering that the singular-plural dichotomy is such a basic feature of both languages and is so often called upon to operate in oral language, the habit of signalling the plural according to the exigencies of each language is one of the most deeply imbedded speech automatisms of English and French speakers. However, as a result of the marked functional difference in announcing the plural in these two languages, it is only through unrelenting practice that a French language learner, more particularly, will succeed in establishing the habit of sounding the plural endings in English and combat the habit, carried over from his mother tongue, of ignoring them.

Another example is the contrastive analysis of the French and English third person singular, present indicative. In French, the first, second, and third person singular of verbs — excluding such verbs as *être* and *avoir* — are the same in the spoken language, whereas in English the third person ends in an /-s/ or /-z/, or has a syllable added to it, /- z/.

French			English		
	(spoken)	(written)		(spoken)	(written)
je	/parl/	(parle-parles)	I	/tɔk/	(talk)
tu	/vwa/	(vois-voit)	you	/si/	(see)
il	/pɛr/	(perd-perds)		/luz/	(lose)
				/tɔks/	(talks)
			he	/siz/	(sees)
				/luzəz/	(loses)

It can be rightly assumed from the above that the French speaker, trained as he is to treat the third person singular in the same way as the other two, will, by virtue of his own linguistic habits and under the influence of analogy, experience some difficulty in establishing the right habit in English.

SYNTACTICAL LEVEL

A contrastive analysis of French and English at the syntactical level would also bring to light structural differences between these two idioms. While *word order,* for example, is a vital linguistic factor common to both French and English, there is by no means a one-to-one correspondence between them. To be sure, word order is meaningful in both languages. *The cat bit the dog* means something different from *The dog bit the cat.* So does *Le chat a mordu le chien* from *Le chien a mordu le chat.* But this is not always the case, for word order does not, in every respect, follow a parallel course in French and English. As an illustration of this, one could point to the difficulty for a French learner of English in overcoming the tendency to say *He speaks well English* instead of *He speaks English well.* One could hardly trace this mistake to any other source but to the linguistic background of the learner. Granted, the wrong arrangement of words, as here exemplified, does not necessarily modify the meaning as radically as in the previous example, neither does it make for standard English. From a practical point of view, a French learner of English would need to engage in specific drills designed to check this particular linguistic interference from his mother tongue.

The *-ing* form in English, to mention another example, is also a source of interference in the learning of English by French speakers. The French language has no such verbal concept as the progressive form which generally expresses duration or action in progress, as in *I am writing* (right now), as opposed to the simple present, which generally expresses an habitual action, as in *I write* (every day). These two notions are rendered in French by means of one single verb form: the present indicative. Only the context will determine whether the action referred to is habitual or progressive. As might be expected, the French speaker is bound to have to devote much time to establishing the automatisms necessary for the proper choice of verb in speech. Not only is the force of habit of his native tongue likely to lead him to use the present instead of the progressive in cases where the latter form is called for, but the very absence of an *-ing* form counterpart in his own vernacular is just as likely to constitute an additional problem.

INTERRELATIONSHIP OF LEVELS

A vital aspect of speech which can be all too easily overlooked in foreign language learning, possibly because of its very elusiveness, is the interrelationship among the three levels of language: phonology, morphology, and syntax. This interlevel relationship, however, is built upon a pre-existing intralevel relationship between units belonging to the same level. In the English word /bats/ *(bats)*, for instance, there is a phonological relationship between the phonemes in so far as each phoneme affects the neighboring one and is affected by it. In /bats/, the /t/ has different phonetic characteristics from the initial /t/ in /tabz/ *(tabs)*, let's say, by virtue of their respective positions (phonetic environment). They are said to be conditioned. This is a case of internal relationship on the phonetic level. The final /s/ in the word /bats/ adds a new dimension — that of plurality or more-than-one — to the lexical one /bat/. As such this /s/ performs a morphological function and is therefore called a morpheme. On the other hand, in the word /bagz/ *(bags)*, the plural notion is expressed by means of the phoneme (morpheme) /z/, owing to the requirements of the phonological system of English, which in this case calls for a /z/ instead of an /s/, after voiced consonant /g/. In this interlocking action resides the close morphophonological relationship between these two levels of structure, i.e., phonology and morphology.

It is worth pointing out, incidentally, that of the many possible rearrangements of the four phonemes /b/, /a/, /t/, and /s/ only two are current in present-day English, to wit, /bats/ and /stab/. *Tabs* is not applicable here since, in the spoken language, the final letter *s* is sounded as /z/, the phonemic spelling being /tabz/. Such hypothetical expressions as: /sabt/, /sbat/, etc., are not part of the English vocabulary. Besides, these sequences of sounds within the boundaries of a word are alien to the English phonological system. It would be difficult indeed to find English words with final consonant clusters such as /-bt/, /-tb/, or with an initial consonant cluster such as /sb-/. But the sequence of sounds /b/-/a/-/t/-/s/ could, conceivably, be rearranged to read /tsab/, by analogy with *tsar*, in which case the consonant cluster /ts/ in initial position would be in accord with the phonological structure of English, even though the word might be claimed to be a foreign importation.

In spite of the wealth of its vocabulary and the great variety of its consonant clusters, the English language has yet to exhaust the possibility of creating new words within the framework of its present phonological system. From a language learning point of view, this has far-reaching implications. Whatever clusters are found in the foreign language and not in the native tongue of the learner may present pronunciation difficulties. It is therefore necessary for the student to practice specific drills or exercises incorporating such clusters so as to train his ear to identify them and his speech organs to utter them.

The interrelationship between phonology and morphology extends to syntax. Using the word *bats* again, we find that the plural signal (morpheme) does affect other parts of the utterance in which it belongs; Example: *Bats are mammals* or *Bats are used in baseball.* In this case the plural signal or morpheme /s/ calls for the plural *are.* These three levels of structure in language are tightly interwoven and a practical knowledge, whether intuitive or conscious, of their interrelationship is a requisite for fluency of speech. In the teaching and learning of a foreign language, however, phonology, morphology, and syntax cannot be divorced or treated as compartmentalized areas of instruction. In actual classroom practice, utterances should be taken up as meaningful wholes and not as isolated forms.

To summarize: Contrastive linguistics serves to remind both the teacher and textbook writer that in foreign language learning, two languages are to be taken into consideration: the target language and the native; that the linguistic habits of the foreign language learner — those of his mother tongue — are already deeply stamped on his subconscious and are bound to resist new habits entering into conflict with older ones; that specific and carefully programmed material designed to overcome the particular linguistic hurdles blocking the way of the learner should be utilized.

THE LANGUAGE LABORATORY

Since speech habits, like all other habits, are acquired only by training and repetition, whatever technical assistance can be brought to the reinforcing of these habits should certainly be employed. Among the more common aids used in language teaching are pictures, flash cards, charts, slides, records, tapes and film strips. However, the most effective technical aid is the language laboratory which allows the student to have individual rapport with the program. It is thus best suited for building the automatisms essential for fluency. In the language laboratory the learner is free to practice privately and in drill form, the matter introduced in class. Whatever material is drilled in the language laboratory must be closely integrated with classroom instruction. Laboratory work should be regarded as an extension of classroom activity: it is essentially the place where language pattern practice becomes speech habit.

Another virtue of the language laboratory is that, in repetitive work, the tape or disc is not subject, as is the human voice, to more or less marked variations from one repetition to another. Also, students are free to proceed at their own individual rates of speed. The more talented ones need not be slowed down to the pace of the class, while the slower ones are not rushed through their work. On the other hand, the timid or self-conscious student who is haunted by the fear of making mistakes develops, within the confines of his booth, more confidence in whatever ability he has for language learning. A single repetition or a small number of repetitions of a pattern cannot, however, be considered sufficient practice for the pattern to become part of the linguistic make-up of the learner. Language learning must necessarily be over-learning.

While the language laboratory is a most precious tool in language learning, the teacher remains the center of importance by virtue of the nature of language. Although basically an aural/oral means of communication, language involves more than just hearing mechanisms. For we do not 'speak' with our vocal organs only; we 'speak' with our whole body. Facial expressions, gestures, shoulder shrugs, motions of the head, a wink, a nod — all of these, under the name of *kinesics,* play a significant part in conveying our thoughts. They not only reinforce speech, but occasionally modify its meaning. A brief utterance such as 'Please' may convey various meanings or shades of meaning depending on the kinesic features accompanying it. Only the human teacher can give full expression to these features.

To be in full command of any linguistic system, whether it be his native language or a foreign tongue, the speaker must be able to use promptly, spontaneously and automatically whatever pattern is required for expressing his thoughts of the moment. It therefore follows that language learning, especially in the early stages, is — and this bears repetition — much more of a mechanical than an intellectual activity. The primary purpose of the language laboratory is, therefore, to help establish the automatisms that make for fluency. Obviously in this process, the intellect is not totally excluded. Its function consists chiefly in selecting the proper word or phrase. To be sure, in such work as transformation and substitution drills, the main object does not so much lie in the selection of the item as in the practicing of the given utterance with the right choice of item. The following example may better illustrate this point.

Let us say that the task at hand is for the French speaker to establish the habit of selecting automatically the right form of the personal pronoun *him* or *her* for the noun in such sentences as: *she saw her brother* (him); *he saw Mary* (her). The learner must practice this type of exercise so thoroughly that the right choice of pronoun is made instantly, without a formal analysis of the linguistic situation, *i.e.,* without any forethought as to whether the noun to be replaced by a pronoun is masculine or feminine, and the pronoun to be substituted for it also masculine or feminine. In other words, any choice to be made that is based on a *conscious* examination of the problem can only be so at the expense of fluency. The mental reactions of the learner must be so automatic that the right selection of *him* or *her,* comes as quickly to his mind and on his lips as the name of the person the pronoun stands for.

A further look into language laboratory learning technique would reveal that, as in classroom instruction, difficulties should be tackled singly and that problem-solving should, as far as possible, be presented so as to elicit the right response from the student. For if speech habits are to be established through repetitious exercises, it is of course imperative that these repetitions be built upon correct responses. More harm than good is likely to result if wrong responses are allowed to be drilled. A form of programmed instruction lends itself nicely to this type of activity, since it breaks down the material to be learned into minimal steps, each step leading, by design, to the next one, no new step being attempted before the previous one has been thoroughly mastered. Also, with this type of instruction, once the learner has given his response, he receives immediate confirmation of his correct answer, and if this answer should be wrong, he is made to correct it at once, so as to give the wrong response as little chance as possible to take root.

Whatever use is made of the language laboratory in foreign language learning, it is essential to bear in mind that it is only an accessory to the task of teaching and learning language. It is not a substitute for classroom instruction. Too many human features are missing from the language laboratory to qualify it as an adequate device for meeting all the requirements of language learning.

---

[1] C. C. Fries, "Advances in Linguistics," *College English,* (Champaign, Ill.: National Council for Teachers of English), Oct. 1961, p. 35.

[2] C. C. Fries, "American Linguistics and the Teaching of English," *Language Learning,* (Ann Arbor, Michigan), VI, 1 and 2, p. 10.

[3] Daniel Jones, *An Outline of English Phonetics* (Cambridge: W. Heffer and Sons, 1956), p. 248.

II THE HISTORICAL BACKGROUND OF LINGUISTICS

Estrella Calimag

LANGUAGE AND LINGUISTICS

Language, which has been considered man's most remarkable achievement, is so much a part of our lives, like the air we breathe, that very often we take it for granted and as often are not aware of its characteristic features. There are many things about language that are still a mystery and will probably remain so. However, there are aspects we do know. The past several decades have seen a tremendous amount of linguistic knowledge that has revolutionized our thinking about the real nature of language. Since the subject matter of linguistics is language, a description of its basic characteristics would make for a better understanding of linguistic science.

Language is a system. It is not a random collection of items. Patterning is all important. There is an underlying pattern in every language, and it is this pattern which the linguist seeks to discover when he sets out to study a language. The system as a whole can be divided into five principal subsystems, three of which are central and two peripheral.

The three central subsystems are: (1) The *grammatical* system: a stock of morphemes, and the arrangements in which they occur; (2) the *phonological* system: a stock of phonemes and the arrangements in which they occur; and (3) the *morphophonemic* system: the code which ties together the grammatical and the phonological systems . . . the two peripheral subsystems are: (4) the *semantic* system, which associates various morphemes, combinations of morphemes, and arrangements in which morphemes can be put, with things and situations, or kinds of things and situations; (5) the *phonetic* system: the way in which sequences of phonemes are converted into sound waves by the articulation of a speaker, and are decoded from the speech signal by a hearer.[1]

Corollary to the systematic nature of language is the uniqueness of this system for each language. Each language has its own structure, its own system. It has its own unique way of organizing its units into an internal structure. This means that each language has its own way of combining its distinctive sounds or phonemes into words and of arranging its words into phrases and sentences. Each unit — phoneme, word, construction — has its own privilege of occurrence peculiar to the language. The phoneme (*ŋg*), for example, occurs both in English and Tagalog (a Philippine language) but has a different distribution in the two languages. In Tagalog /ŋg/ occurs in initial (*ngayon*-now), medial (*pangalan*-name) and final (*galang*-respect) positions; in English it occurs in medial *(singer)* and final *(bring)* but not in initial position. The common pattern for an English sentence is NV (noun - verb); for Tagalog it is VN *(tumakbo ang aso* — Ran the dog, i.e. The dog ran). English is stress-timed; Tagalog is syllable-timed; that is, each syllable receives the same degree of stress. English has nine vowel phonemes (depending on the idiolect on which analysis is based); Tagalog and most Philippine languages have a three-vowel system basically. In the area of vocabulary and meaning, languages differ, too. Gaddang, a minor Philippine language, has four forms corresponding to the form *and* in English. In short, no two languages are alike. Language is therefore idio-syncratic.

Language is a set of sounds. These sounds are vocal, that is, they are produced by the human organs of speech — lips, tongue, larynx, etc. Sounds make up the raw materials of language. It is these sounds that language employs to carry its message. Other sounds — sirens, drum beats, whistles — also have meaning but these are not sounds produced by the human speech mechanism and therefore are not linguistic symbols. While man is capable of making hundreds of varieties of sounds, only a few of these are distinctive or relevant. The number of these distinctive sounds or phonemes for each language has been put between twenty and seventy. The sounds produced by the vocal organs are of two types: consonants and vowels. Consonants are produced by making some obstruction (by the lips, tongue, etc.) along the path of the breath stream as it journeys from the lungs to the outside, while vowels are shaped by the formation of resonance chambers in the mouth and nose.

Language is a set of symbols which means that language has meaning. "The meaning of a form is described in terms of the situations in which it is used, i.e. in terms of its ethnolinguistic environment."[2] The ethnolinguistic environment of form consists of two contexts: linguistic — the positions which a form may occupy in the structure of the language; and nonlinguistic — the cultural context in which the form occurs.[3] The utterances made by speakers of a language have meanings which are related to objects and events in the objective world. A form in one context means one thing and in another context may mean something else. One word or phrase in one language may cover a semantic range requiring more than one verbal equivalent in another language and vice versa. Closely related to the meaningfulness of linguistic symbols is the arbitrariness of the symbols themselves; that is, there is no inherent or natural relationship between a word and its referent or what it stands for. For example, there is nothing horselike about the word *horse*. The word for *dog* in Tagalog is *aso*; in Spanish it is *perro*; in French it is *chien*; in German it is *hund*. Other languages use other words. It is convention, agreement among the members of a speech community, that assigns meaning to a word.

Language has form which consists of a combination of distinctive sounds or phonemes. Linguistic forms are either bound or free. A form is free if it can occur by itself as with *boy* in *boyish*. It is bound if it cannot occur by itself as with *ish* in *boyish*.

Language does not operate in a vacuum. It is an integral part of culture, and like culture, it is learned behavior. Language is at the very core of culture itself. Indeed, one discovers many features of culture reflected in language. ". . . Language is felt to be a perfect symbolic system, in a perfectly homogeneous medium, for the handling of all references and meanings that a given culture is capable of, whether these be in the form of actual communications or in that of such ideal substitutes of communication as thinking. The content of every culture is expressible in its language . . . ."[4]

Each language is perfectly adequate for the speech community which uses it. Languages of primitive societies are just as highly developed as those of sophisticated societies. It might be pointed out that many of the little known languages of the world have a structure more complex than those of the world's "great" languages. We may label certain societies as primitive; we can not use the same label for any language. Tagalog is an excellent language for expressing Filipino culture; American English is an excellent language for communicating American culture but would be a poor one for expressing Bantu culture.

Language changes. This is a natural and normal process. People change. Times change. The English of 1600 would be relatively unintelligible to us today. The English of 900 would be foreign. Linguistic change occurs on all levels — phonological, grammatical, semantic, and lexical. The phonemes /ž/ and /ŋ/ in Modern English did not occur in Middle English. Middle English /hu:s/ has become Modern English /haws/. Modern English has a system of gender based on sex, Old English had a grammatical gender. Only a few of the many inflectional categories in Old English survive in Modern English. Words change meaning all the time. The semantic range of a word may go up or down the moral scale. For example, until 1200, the word *wench* meant a child of either sex. *Barter* formerly meant deceive. Now it is up the ladder. *Cunning* formerly meant knowing, now it means "crooked" knowing. Lexical items appear and disappear from the linguistic scene. Many new items have come into being within the past few years — *sputnik, fallout, go-go, frug, mod* — to mention only a few.

Finally, the main *raison d'être* of language is communication.

The property of language which renders it such a powerful means of communication is that one can say something that has never been said before, and yet be perfectly understood, often without either speaker or audience being aware of the novelty. A novel utterance is built from familiar raw-materials, by familiar patterns of putting raw-materials together. Neither the raw-materials nor the patterns need be new in order for the utterance to be different from any that has occurred previously.[5]

We can now define language as a structured system of arbitrary vocal symbols by means of which members of a speech community communicate.

LINGUISTIC RESEARCH

Language, the subject matter of linguistics, has a history as old as man himself. Archeological evidence points to the antiquity of man's most unique accomplishment. Clay tablets, discovered in a Sumerian city named Erech and believed to be among the world's first written documents, contain word lists apparently intended for study and practice. Thus, it would seem that as early as 3000 B.C. some Sumerian scribes were already thinking in terms of language teaching and learning.[6]

Interest in language and in questions relating to its nature has continued down the centuries. The ancient Greeks speculated about language, or more specifically, about the Greek language, which to them was the ideal and most logical tongue. Plato's works, especially the *Cratylus*, contain his views on the nature of language. Plato contended that there was a natural relationship between a word and its referent. Aristotle, on the other hand, asserted that the relationship between a word and the object for which it stood in the practical world was completely arbitrary. The latter view is held by linguists today. The ancient Greeks were also interested in the fundamental aspects of grammar. This is evidenced in the works of the famous Greek grammarians of the day — Dionysius Thrax, Appollonius Dyscolus, and Herodian. They described the main syntactic and inflectional forms of their language. Plato made the distinction between a noun and a verb. Aristotle proposed the term conjunction. The Stoics thought that, since matter consisted of four elements, there must be four parts of speech. Eight parts of speech were finally posited — noun, verb, pronoun, participle, adverb, preposition, conjunction, and article. It must be noted that the formulations made by the ancient Greeks concerning language were based on philosophical considerations rather than on what was directly observable in the linguistic data.

When Greek culture spread across the Roman world, the Romans adopted wholesale the statements which the Greeks made about the Greek language. It was a case of forcing the pattern of Latin to fit into the mold of Greek. (Incidentally, we see traces of this phenomenon in many grammar books of our day. The labels for form classes and grammatical categories and relationships which the Romans inherited from the Greeks were handed down to us. Until recently all descriptions of English grammar were couched in terms duplicating those used in Latin grammars of ancient times.) The Romans, who frequently deplored the "poverty" of their own language compared with the magnificence of Greek, were the first to use a foreign language systematically to increase their mastery over their own.[7] Roman students did translations from Greek into Latin and vice versa, while their teachers laid the foundations for the traditional comparative grammar as they analyzed the works of Cicero and Demosthenes, Homer and Virgil. While Latin was the official language, Greek with its great prestige continued to flourish in the East, so that the Roman Empire was in effect bilingual. Aristocratic young Romans learned to speak Greek naturally from a Greek slave almost before they learned Latin; but as Greek began to decline from about the second century A.D., more artificial methods — including bilingual textbooks — came into use.

Meanwhile in another part of the world, towards the end of the fourth century B.C., Panini, the celebrated Indian grammarian had been hard at work on what was to become one of the most comprehensive descriptive analyses of any language. Panini's Sanskrit grammar was a descriptive study in the modern linguistic sense. (In the nineteenth century, this work exerted a great influence on the development of historical and comparative linguistics.) After the collapse of the Roman Empire, Greek all but disappeared in Western Europe; linguistic activity during the Medieval Period centered around the study of Latin grammar, especially in the works of Priscian and Donatus.

The Renaissance brought with it important effects on linguistic scholarship. Classical Greek was rediscovered and the study of Hebrew and Arabic introduced. The spread of Christianity and the era of historical discoveries and explorations resulted in the accumulation of a great body of data on language outside Europe. Among the early linguistic works during this period were word and phrase lists designed to help travelers to distant places and missionaries in strange lands. In addition to compiling word lists, missionaries also wrote grammars of exotic tongues. These grammars, to be sure, were patterned after Latin and therefore were not scientifically constructed.

Although the years of discoveries and explorations, the invention of the printing press, and general scientific inquiry resulted in the widening of the linguistic horizon, the observations made on language up to this point were not much different from those put forward in classical times.

The intellectual climate during the eighteenth century brought out live issues relating to languages. Among the popular issues were those relating to semantic structure, language function, and linguistic typology. It was not until 1786, however, that a turning point in linguistic scholarship came about. Sir William Jones, working for the British government in India, publicly made the statement that the correspondences he had observed among Sanskrit, Latin, and Greek were too striking and regular to be attributed to mere chance. This observation led him to the conclusion that these three languages were related and were descended from the same source. This statement sparked the movement that was to become the main preoccupation of linguists during the nineteenth century.

The nineteenth century was the age of *historical and comparative linguistics*. Linguists of this period were very much interested in establishing genetic relationships among languages. Many investigations of the Indo-European family of languages were undertaken. Rasmus Rask's *Investigation on the Origin of the Old Norse or Icelandic Language*, published in 1818, marked the beginning of scientific comparative linguistics. Jakob Grimm's second volume of *Deutsche Grammatik*, published in 1822, dealt with the systematic correspondences of consonants between Germanic and other Indo-European languages. These correspondences in sound change came to be known as Grimm's Law. Exceptions to these correspondences were at length noticed and it was Verner in 1875 who provided the rule to account for what seemed to be an exception to the regularity of change observed by Grimm. Other great linguists of the nineteenth century also wrote comparative grammars and dictionaries of the Indo-European languages. Towards the end of the century a group of linguists who were called neogrammarians vigorously pursued the notion of the regularity of sound change stemming from Verner's works.

The dawn of *structural linguistics*[8] in the twentieth century did not mean the end of studies in historical and comparative linguistics. Structural-descriptive linguistics was an outgrowth of linguistic activities in the nineteenth century and the advances linguistics has made have been due to the concerted efforts of European, British, and American scholars. In Europe three names deserve mention for pioneering efforts in linguistic scholarship. The Swiss linguist mentioned earlier, Ferdinand de Saussure, has been called the precursor of modern descriptive linguistics.

De Saussure made two distinctions which have helped to delineate the subject matter of linguistics: (1) the *signifiant*, or concept, and the *signifié*, or expression; and (2) *la parole*, or the speech act, and *la langue*, the abstract linguistic system. He also distinguished between synchronic and diachronic studies and proposed that the two, being distinct, should be handled separately and differently.[9]

In America two independent trends converged to provide the nucleus of the American school of linguistics. Towards the end of the nineteenth century, W.D. Whitney, a professor of Sanskrit studies at Yale University, was responsible for making historical linguistics a part of linguistic activity in America. Early in the twentieth century, Franz Boas, a great anthropologist-linguist, provided the groundwork for the study of Amerindian languages and in 1911 published *A Handbook of American Indian Languages* which became a standard guide for anthropologists as well as linguists. E. Sapir, a student of Boas, also worked on American Indian languages. His *Language*, published in 1921, is now considered a classic. Some people, indeed, associate the birth of modern linguistics in America with Sapir.

The great moving force in American descriptive linguistics was Leonard Bloomfield whose *Language* (1933) was for a long time considered the bible of linguistics. This book had a great influence on linguistic activity in America just as de Saussure's *Cours* had in Europe. *Language*, according to a more recent assessment,

summarized the whole field as it had developed up to that time — descriptive, historical, and geographical. Not only did he (Bloomfield) work these divergent approaches together into a remarkably consistent presentation but he made in the book a number of brilliant and productive innovations.[10]

Linguistic research after Bloomfield was devoted to refining the methods and techniques of linguistic analysis which he had put forth. The years after 1933 saw the elaboration and refinement of the theories and methods stated in *Language*. So strong was Bloomfield's influence, that this period has come to be referred to as the "Bloomfieldian era" in American linguistics. At this time however other key figures produced works that were to form the mainstay of American linguistics. Among these were Kenneth Pike, one of the country's greatest phoneticians, Eugene Nida, often called "Mr. Morphology," Bernard Bloch, Zellig Harris, Charles F. Hockett, George Trager, and Henry Lee Smith, Jr.

Linguistics in America before World War II was devoted largely to the study of American Indian languages. Boas, Sapir and Bloomfield did extensive work in the field. The outbreak of World War II brought a temporary halt to pursuit of linguistic research, especially to the interchange of ideas between American linguists and their European counterparts. The War also brought about a great need for the study of many "crucial" languages which had never been taught on this continent before. Language teaching up to that point had been carried on through the grammar-translation method. Success with this approach was minimal. To help with the emergency, the services of expert linguists were engaged. These linguists made preliminary analyses of the languages and their analyses became the basis for the construction of text materials.

World War II thus marked a significant stage in the development of linguistic research in America. Among its most tide-turning effects was a revolutionized outlook on foreign language teaching. To be sure, linguists such as Whitney and Bloomfield had earlier shown some interest in language teaching but it was not until the United States entered the war that an urgent need for better foreign language teaching was felt. Under the leadership of C. C. Fries, the application of the findings of modern linguistic research to language learning and teaching was begun.

The end of the war saw modern descriptive linguistics making inroads into the area of language teaching which marked the birth of *applied linguistics*. The success of the defense language program engendered interest and encouraged language teachers to adopt the methods used for the schools.

In the period following the end of World War II there was an influx of foreign students into the United States. This was part of the cultural exchange program between the U.S.A. and many foreign nations. There was also a steady increase in the number of immigrants coming to America. These two groups of foreigners necessitated the organization of classes for the teaching of English as a second language. Other developments led to the expansion of the application of linguistics to language learning and teaching. The National Defense Education Act of 1958 made possible the growth of research on "neglected languages" and on the preparation of language teaching materials based on the findings of linguistic research. The Center for Applied Linguistics was established by the Modern Language Association. The Center has since served as a clearing house for the dissemination of information related to applied linguistics both in America and abroad.

SCHOLARSHIP TRENDS

The end of the war also reopened the channels of communication between European and American linguists. This, of course, again made possible the exchange of ideas between the two groups. Postwar years also saw further refinement of the Bloomfieldian tradition and the eventual emergence of several different approaches to linguistics problems. Trends which had their beginnings in Europe found some following in the United States. The years after the war were spent largely in the refinement of discovery procedures on all levels of structure: phonology, morphology, and syntax. Discovery procedures, particularly in phonology were thoroughly worked out. These involved segmentation and classification of linguistic units and, in phonology, the establishment of phonemes based on the criteria of phonetic similarity and distinction. The same techniques employed for discovering the phonemes of a language were also used for the identification of morphemes. The approach in the area of syntax was largely the "immediate constituent" (IC) which analyzed a construction in terms of two parts, its immediate constituents, as it were. For example, *The new girl lives down the block* would be divided into *The new girl* and *lives down the block*, these two parts being the IC's of the whole sentence.

Each IC, in turn, is cut into two and so on until the ultimate constituents, the morphemes, of which the sentence is made are reached. This approach was much favored and produced a number of variants of the IC. Activities were on an even keel through the early 50's until 1957 when another turning point was reached.

During this year, Noam Chomsky published his now celebrated *Syntactic Structures* in which he delineated a novel approach to syntactic description. In his view, a grammar consists of three components: syntactic, semantic and phonological,[11] and his treatment provides for two main types of rules for the generation of sentences. Phrase-structure rules generate kernel sentences, a finite number of simple, active, declarative sentences which form the core of a language. Transformational rules are those which are applied to the kernel sentences to produce all the other sentences in the language. The phrase-structure rules provide the deep structure of a sentence while the transformational rules provide the surface structure. The semantic component of the grammar relates to the deep structure, giving meaning to the sentence. The phonological component relates to the surface structure, giving the sentence its pronunciation. Chomsky proposes a procedure for approximating the native speaker's innate ability to form grammatical sentences of varying degrees of complexity even though he had never made these utterances before. In this approach the question is not which groups of words in the sentence are more closely related to each other but rather what utterance is another utterance related to. It is the relationship, for instance, of an active sentence to a passive one, an affirmative to a negative, a statement to a question, that transformational grammar, as this approach is called, tries to explain.

Transformational grammar has been the focus of a great deal of debate and controversy since it was first introduced in May 1957. Many former structuralists have jumped onto the TG (transformational grammar) band wagon and have vigorously tried to show that this theory is a definite improvement over those that held the field until 1957. Among those who have come under Chomsky's influence are Halle, Postal, Lees, and Stockwell. The transformationalists have reason to put forth strong claims as to the efficacy of their theory. It has been shown that the TG approach is very effective in resolving ambiguity. One big drawback, however, is its seeming preoccupation with abstract algebraic notation which takes the material out of the comprehension range of the not-too-mathematically-inclined.

Another approach to linguistic description deserves mention since a great deal of research, especially in the area of Mexican-Indian languages, has been done within its framework. The tagmemic approach, as it is called was pioneered by Pike and his colleagues at the Summer Institute of Linguistics and is almost contemporaneous with the TG theory. The basic concept in tagmemics is the "tagmeme" which refers to the correlation of a class of items, each item of which can be substituted for another. Hence, a certain slot, say a subject slot, is filled by a certain class.[12]

Linguistics is, indeed, in a state of ferment. There are a number of seemingly rival linguistic theories. The formidable array of technical terms is enough to baffle the student and, sometimes, there seems to be more discord than unity. Yet, for all the disagreements, there are many areas of concord. It is evident from the growing body of literature that several lines of inquiry are being followed. Much still needs to be refined and systematized but it is gratifying to note that the gap between the divergent views is narrowing. This is a hopeful sign.

---

[1] Charles F. Hockett, *A Course in Modern Linguistics* (New York: The Macmillan Company, 1958), pp. 137-138.

[2] Eugene Nida, "A System for the Description of Semantic Elements," *Word,* VII (April, 1951), p. 4.

[3] *Ibid.*, pp. 4-5.

[4] Edward Sapir, *Culture, Language and Personality,* ed. by G. Mandelbaum (Berkeley: University of California Press, 1957), p. 6.

[5] Charles F. Hockett, *op.cit.,* p. 157.

[6] Cf. Samuel Noah Kramer, *From the Tablets of Sumer* (Indian Hills, Colorado: Falcon's Wing Press, 1956), pp. 3-9.

[7] Cf. H. I. Marrou, *A History of Education in Antiquity.* George Lamb, (trans.). (London: Sheed and Ward, 1956), p. 255.

[8]Structural-descriptive linguistics is used to refer to "The kind of linguistics which is primarily interested in discovering and describing as concisely and accurately as possible the interrelationships and patterns which make up the intricate structures of languages. In a way, structural linguistics can be called the mathematics of language study because it is likely to be rather abstract and preoccupied with methods." W. Nelson Francis, *The Structure of American English* (New York: The Ronald Press Co., 1958), p. 26.

[9]For other European and British contributions, see Introduction.

[10]H. A. Gleason, Jr., *Linguistics and English Grammar* (New York: Holt, Rinehart and Winston, Inc., 1965), pp. 46-47.

[11]For a detailed discussion of this theory see Noam Chomsky, *Aspects of the Theory of Syntax* (Cambridge, Mass: The M. I. T. Press, 1965) and *Cartesian Linguistics* (New York: Harper and Row, 1966).

[12]For an introduction to tagmemics, see Benjamin Elson and Vilma Pickett, *An Introduction to Morphology and Syntax* (Santa Ana, California: Summer Institute of Linguisitcs, 1944).

III

BILINGUALISM AND THE TEACHER OF ENGLISH AS A FOREIGN LANGUAGE

L. Bruce Barkman

The teacher of English as a foreign language is very likely to find himself in a country where a bilingual or multilingual situation exists. The English teacher who goes to Guinea may find that his students are already bilingual in French and one or more of several African languages, perhaps Fula or Susu. In Paraguay, students of English will probably be bilingual in Spanish and Guarani. Haitian learners of English will know French and Haitian Creole. Bilingual communities are not uncommon even in countries that use English for most purposes and whose populations consist largely of native speakers of English. Some bilingual communities in English-speaking countries were in existence before those countries had developed their political identities. These communities have retained their original languages and have added English. A few examples are the Welsh and Gaelic bilingual communities in Great Britain, the French in Canada, and the Pennsylvania German in the United States.

Bilingualism affects the languages in contact, bilingual individuals, and the sociocultural setting. It often has considerable bearing on the political and economic decisions of nations. Investigators from a number of disciplines and two subdisciplines, psycholinguistics and sociolinguistics, have examined various aspects of bilingualism. Linguists have provided models of bilingual description for the classification of the kinds of interference and language change resulting from language contact.

They have attempted to predict areas of interference on the basis of structural differences between the languages. They have also made hypotheses concerning the organization of the linguistic systems that bilinguals may have in their heads on the basis of the utterances that these individuals produce. Psychologists have tested the linguists' hypotheses, studied the effects of bilingualism on intelligence, and have attempted to discover how language aptitude and different motivations influence the acquisition of satisfactory bilingual behavior. Sociologists and educators, among others, are concerned with the functions of each language in a bilingual situation and the popular and official attitudes toward those functions and the languages themselves. Politicians and economists must often make decisions affecting language function and the future development of their countries. Their decisions depend on such factors as national pride, the necessity for technical assistance from abroad, the need for immediate widespread expansion of the educational system, and the presence or absence of accurate information concerning the bilingual situation.

If English is one of the languages in a bilingual country, it may have functions of varying relative importance with respect to other languages in that country. In the United States, English is the only language used for official purposes, the language of instruction in all public and most private schools. It is used overwhelmingly for business, correspondence of all sorts, entertainment, education and practically the entire population speaks English natively. It seems reasonable to state that English is dominant over the other languages used in the United States.

In India, however, English is used as an administrative and business language, and for higher education. It has official status along with Hindi, and sometimes serves as a language of wider communication in the country, but almost no one speaks English natively. However, in 1966, when officials attempted to displace English as an official language in favor of Hindi alone, reactions were so strong that both had to be retained as official languages. Although English has important functions in India, it does not have the all-important role played by English in the United States.

In Puerto Rico, Spanish is the language most often used for official purposes, although English has at least a nominal official role. Three quarters of the population are native speakers of

Spanish and Spanish is used for practically all aspects of life, but because of Puerto Rico's particular relationship to the United States, English was used for a number of years (1905-1916) as the sole medium of instruction in the public schools; it is now taught as a special subject for ninety minutes a day. English is also used there as one of the languages of instruction at the university level. A Puerto Rican with a good command of English usually has a relatively high socioeconomic status with respect to non-English speaking Puerto Ricans, but attitudes toward English vary considerably. In some newly developing nations, the only function that English may serve is as a way to keep abreast of technological advances outside the countries.

The teacher of English as a foreign language is trying to induce bilingual behavior in his students. He should have a basic theoretical understanding of useful models of bilingual description so that he can analyze his students' errors adequately and either find or write suitable lessons to help correct them. He should be familiar with his students' motivations for achieving bilingualism and their language learning aptitudes so that he can change his materials and methods if necessary. The functions of English in a given sociocultural setting will undoubtedly have a strong influence on the way it should be taught. The student who has to do graduate work with English as the medium of instruction or who plans to specialize in English literature needs a different set of skills from the student who will use English only as a means of access to technical articles. An awareness of some of the popular and official attitudes toward bilingualism and the functions of English should make it possible for the teacher of English to analyze his particular situation and work within it efficiently and effectively.

BILINGUALISM AND LINGUISTICS

The investigation of any discipline necessitates the development of definitions and the rest of the apparatus appropriate to the description and analysis of that discipline. Linguists have developed such an apparatus for the description and analysis of bilingual phenomena. An acquaintance with the framework of bilingual investigation should enable the teacher of English as a foreign language to analyze and act upon the particular problems related to bilingualism that he is bound to encounter in the classroom.

Over the years, linguists have proposed a number of definitions of bilingualism and of bilingual individuals. One of these, the "native-like control over two languages,"[1] corresponds fairly closely to popular notions concerning bilingual behavior. This definition implies that the bilingual individual has a high level of proficiency in both of his languages, that he can use each language equally well for any purpose, and that he has an equal ability to understand and produce spoken and written information in both languages. Observers of individuals who use more than one language note that practically no one can meet the requirements of such a definition. Professional translators often state that they translate into one of their languages more easily than into the other. Individuals who use different languages for different topics tend to have a lesser degree of proficiency if they attempt to use the "wrong" language for a given topic. For example, a Puerto Rican schoolchild in New York may have difficulty talking about his home (where Spanish is spoken) if he is asked to do so at school (where English is spoken). A common observation of the children and grandchildren of immigrants in the U.S.A. is that although they understand the language of their parents and grandparents, they speak it badly, if at all, and can neither read nor write it.

In another definition, proposed by Haugen in 1953, bilingualism begins "at the point where the speaker of one language can produce *complete, meaningful utterances* in the other language."[2] It does not specify a high level of proficiency or an equal ability in both languages, although it does require that the bilingual individual be able to produce utterances in the other language. Haugen later dropped all proficiency requirements, and defined bilingual as ". . . a cover term for people with a number of different language skills, having in common only that they are not monolinguals. A *monolingual . . .* is a person who knows only one language."[3] The later definition, while distinguishing bilinguals from monolinguals, does not specify what bilingual behavior is.

In 1953, Weinreich defined bilingualism as "the practice of alternately using two languages."[4] This definition seems more satisfactory than the other since degree of proficiency, equal ability, and specification of passive or active language skills for each language are not involved. This is not to say that linguists are not interested in different kinds and degrees of bilingualism. On the contrary, most linguistic investigations of bilingual situations have treated just such differences at some length.[5] However, Weinreich's definition makes it possible to include a wide range of language behavior under the term bilingualism. Any alternate use of two languages, either by individuals or by communities, will be considered a case of bilingualism in the present chapter. The alternate use of more than two languages is correctly called multilingualism, but for convenience will be here treated as bilingualism.

INTERFERENCE

The bilingual individual brings his languages into contact. All human languages have many of the same functions and the bilingual often identifies the sounds, lexical items, syntactic structures, and meanings of one of his languages with equivalent units in his other language. A Spanish-English bilingual may formulate an identification between Spanish nouns ending in -*ción*, such as *nación, revelación,* and *abstracción,* and English nouns ending in -*tion*, such as *nation, revelation,* and *abstraction*. But the bilingual must take care not to apply this identification to all Spanish words ending in -*ción*, because he may produce what he thinks are English forms, say "califaction" (from Spanish *califacción*), which in English is *central heating*. Whenever a bilingual produces a form in a language which a monolingual speaker of that language would not use, either as a result of identification or other reasons, a case of *interference* has occurred. Few bilinguals are able to keep their languages completely free from interference, although many try to avoid it by switching from one language to the other, if they are uncertain of their ability to keep them separate in a specific instance.

Linguists explain interference phenomena in terms of the structural differences between the languages. Interference may arise at any level — phonological, morphological, syntactic, or semantic — where the bilingual's languages differ in structure. Linguists generally evaluate the relative skills of bilinguals according to the quantity of interference manifested in their use of each language. A bilingual who evidences a great amount of interference in one or more of his languages is rated as having little skill. It is sometimes possible to predict the form that interference will take on the basis of a comparison of the structural differences in the languages, especially at the phonological level. However, interference cannot be explained wholly in terms of the structural differences between the languages in question, because bilinguals of two given languages do not manifest the same interference phenomena. For example, some varieties of Spanish have a palatal nasal phoneme /ñ/, as in /señór/, which is nonexistent in English. The nearest English phonological equivalent is a sequence of an alveolar nasal and a palatal semivowel, /ny/ , as in /sínyər/ *senior*. An English-Spanish bilingual should produce the English sequence /ny/ for Spanish /ñ/, if interference occurs, and many of them do just that. But some English speakers of Spanish produce English /n/ or /ŋ/ (a velar nasal) instead. At a given point of structural difference in two languages, interference may take more than one form, as described in the above example. If all the forms of interference cannot be accounted for in terms of the structural differences in the two languages, it will be necessary to consider nonlinguistic factors in order to explain some of the forms of interference. Some of the psychological and cultural factors involved in interference phenomena will be discussed below.

In bilingual communities, interference invariably results in structural changes in at least one of the languages, and sometimes in both.[6] These changes, commonly called *diffusion* or *borrowing,* occur when the speakers of one of the languages accept any manifestation of interference as appropriate for regular use in the other language. The teacher of English as a foreign language is normally interested in the prevention or correction of interference and diffusion, but in order to do so as economically as possible, he should be able to recognize the sorts of interference his students produce. The terminology devised to describe the kinds of diffusion resulting from interference provides a useful analytical framework that the teacher of English can follow in his analysis of student errors. The *lending* or *donor language* is the language which furnishes the diffused items. The language which borrows the items is known as the *recipient language.* A borrowed item, as it exists in the lending language, is called the *model.* In the recipient language, a borrowed item is referred to as the *replica.* Structural resemblances between the model and the replica are described as *importations,* whereas differences between the model and the replica are treated as *substitutions.*[7] One of the necessities of an accurate analysis of interference phenomena in terms of structural differences between the recipient and donor languages is accurate descriptions of both of the languages. Although it is not absolutely necessary for the descriptions of the languages to have the same form, say transformational, it is easier to analyze interference if they do have the same form.

PHONOLOGICAL INTERFERENCE

Phonological interference may be described as phonetic, phonemic, allophonic, or distributional. The investigator must know the sounds of both the donor and recipient languages, the organization of the sounds into phonemes, and the distribution of the phonemes in utterances. The classification of the different types of phonological interference given below follows that outlined by Moulton.[8]

One source of phonological interference may result if the donor language has a phoneme with one major allophone and the recipient language has a structurally similar phoneme with one major allophone that is phonetically different. For example, Spanish has a mid-back rounded vowel, as does English, but English /o/ is phonetically different from its Spanish counterpart, because it has a prominent upward back glide. When the Spanish speaker speaks English, he produces English words such as *no, goat,* and *sown* with his unglided vowel. The identification of his Spanish phoneme with the phonetically different English one has resulted in a case of phonetic interference. This kind of phonetic interference seldom leads to misunderstanding, although it certainly contributes to foreign accent.

If the recipient language has a phoneme which does not exist in the donor language, the bilingual will tend to equate the phoneme in the recipient language with the phonetically most similar phoneme in the donor language. Thus, a speaker of Canadian French will produce English /θ/ as /t/, and /ð/ as /d/ in words such as *ether, breath, either,* and *this.* A Frenchman who demonstrates interference for English /θ/ and /ð/, however, identifies them with his /s/ and /z/ phonemes. There may be a structural explanation for the lack of accord in the identifications made by French Canadians and Frenchmen with respect to English /θ/ and /ð/, since their varieties of French differ considerably as to the phonetic qualities of the allophones of /t/, /d/, /s/, and /z/, but it is worth pointing out that bilinguals do not necessarily make the same phonemic identifications, even if they speak varieties of the same language natively. This kind of phonemic interference may cause misunderstanding as well as contribute to prominent foreign accent, because of the minimal contrasts which exist in the recipient language. The identification of English /ð/ with Canadian French /d/ will result in sentences such as /hìnìdzdəlǽdər/, which will be interpreted by a native English speaker either as *He needs the lather* or *He needs the ladder.* If the donor language has a phoneme which does not exist in the recipient language, interference problems usually do not arise, as long as no phonemic identifications are made. To continue with the preceding example, the native speaker of English simply does not use /θ/ and /ð/ when he speaks French.

Another source of phonemic interference may arise if the donor language has two phones, say Spanish [d] and [ð], which are allophones of a single phoneme, /d/. The recipient language also has the phones [d] and [ð], which are separate phonemes, as in English. The Spanish speaker will identify the English phonemes /d/ and /ð/ as allophones of a single phoneme, and will carry over to English the distribution that those phones have in Spanish. Depending on the specific English words, this kind of interference may be overt or covert. If the Spanish speaker uses words like *dandy, other,* or *breathe,* he will use phones which approximate those appropriate to English and interference will remain covert. If he uses words like *adder* or *breed,* however, he will use Spanish [ð] where English /d/ is appropriate, because only [ð] can occur in those positions in Spanish, and the interference becomes overt. The converse of this variety of interference, in which the donor language has two phones belonging to two phonemes, whereas the recipient language groups the same phones into a single phoneme, will not cause any misunderstanding. Interference remains covert, although Weinreich suggests that overcareful pronunciation of the sounds in question may be considered an overt sign of interference.[9]

A further source of phonemic interference is the existence of a sequence of phonemes in the donor language which is a single phoneme in the recipient language. For example, French has the phonemes /t/ and /ʃ/, which may occur in sequence in items like *tchèque,* /tʃɛk/ and *match,* /matʃ/. English also also has the phonemes /t/ and /ʃ/, which occur in sequence in expressions like *white shoes* /waɪt ʃuz/, and as a single phoneme in expressions like *why choose,* /wâɪ čúz/. The Frenchman speaking English is unable to differentiate such minimal pairs. Furthermore, since the sequence /tʃ/ has a low functional load in French (i.e., it occurs in very few lexical items and differentiates few minimal pairs), the Frenchman may equate English /č/ not with French /tʃ/ but with French /ʃ/, and produce English *cheap,* /čip/ as /ʃip/, *witch,* /wɪč/ as /wɪʃ/ and the like, thus causing considerable misunderstanding.

A case of allophonic interference may occur when a phoneme of the donor language has an allophone which is not shared by a corresponding phoneme in the recipient language. In English, there are two major allophones of /1/. One of them is fairly similar to Spanish /1/ in that the tongue tip and blade are in contact with the alveolar ridge, the rest of the tongue is raised toward the hard palate, and the air stream escapes through a narrow passage at the sides. This allophone of English /1/ occurs in syllable-initial position and sometimes intervocalically, as in *leap, lily.* The allophone of English /1/ which occurs in syllable-final position and before consonants, as in *ill, filthy,* is quite different. The tongue tip barely touches the alveolar ridge and the rest of the tongue is raised toward the soft palate. If the English speaker uses this second allophone of /1/ in Spanish words such as *Helga* and *col,* Spanish speakers will consider him to have a strong foreign accent and may even interpret that allophone of /1/ as Spanish /u/. If Spanish is the donor language and English the recipient language, a similar situation obtains for Spanish allophones of /y/, which results in the production of English /y/ as [ʒ] or [dʒ], as in [dʒélo] for English *yellow.*

Another kind of allophonic interference arises if a phoneme in the donor language never has allophones like those of the corresponding phonemes in the recipient language. Beyond this, the phoneme in the donor language has two allophones, one of which is even more phonetically different from the recipient language phoneme than the other. For example, English /t/ has as two of its allophones *a fortis* (relatively tense articulation and strong expiration) aspirated apico-alveolar stop [tʰ] and *a lenis* (lax articulation and weak expiration) apico-alveolar flap [ɾ]. The aspirated allophone occurs in syllable-initial position, and the flapped allophone before an unstressed vowel. Spanish /t/ is dental and unaspirated. The English allophone [tʰ] may be used instead of the unaspirated Spanish allophone, even though this interference produces an effect of heavy foreign accent. But the flapped allophone of English /t/ is so different from any allophone of Spanish /t/, and so similar to Spanish /r/, that the Spanish speaker may interpret an English rendition of *bata* as *bara*, *foto* as *foro*, and the like.

Differences in the distribution of the phonemes of the donor and recipient languages also cause interference. Distributional differences are described in terms of the positions that phonemes occupy and the sequences that they participate in relative to other phonemes in utterances. Only a few of the possibilities will be discussed here. One distributional difference which is likely to cause interference is the presence of a corresponding phoneme in both the donor language and the recipient language. The corresponding phonemes occur in syllable-initial position in the recipient language, but not in the donor language. French regularly permits /ʒ/ in syllable-initial position, but English does not. So the English speaker of French will have difficulty in identifying his own /ʒ/ with French /ʒ/ in syllable-initial position, and will tend to substitute English /dʒ/ in that position. Similar problems arise for syllable-final and other positions. For example, English permits voiceless stops in final position with great frequency, as in *hip, hit,* and *hick.* Spanish rarely if ever permits voiceless stops before silence. When the Spanish speaker attempts to produce words ending in voiceless stops, he either leaves them off altogether, or, more rarely, adds a voiceless vocalic release, so that *heat* becomes [hi] or [hitə̥].

Another kind of distributional interference occurs when both the donor and recipient languages have corresponding phonemes, but only the recipient language permits their use in sequence. Spanish and English share /p/, /r/, and /w/ phonemes, but only Spanish permits their sequential use, as in /prwéba/. The English speaker of Spanish regularly reproduces this as [pruéba], changing the semi-consonant to a vowel, or as [préba], eliminating the semi-consonant and reducing the consonant cluster to conform with English norms. Sometimes the donor and recipient languages have the same permitted sequences or corresponding phonemes, but the recipient language permits the sequences in utterance positions not allowed by the donor language. For example, both English and Spanish permit the consonant sequences /sp/, /st/, and /sk/. The English sequences may occur in initial position, as in *spade, star,* and *ski,* but the Spanish sequences may occur only after a vowel, as in *espada, estar,* and *esquina.* The Spanish speaker of English may manifest interference in a number of ways. He may say [ɛspéd] [ɛstár], and [ɛskí], he may drop the initial /s/ of the English clusters, or, if he comes from certain parts of the Spanish-speaking world, he may transfer his [h] allophone of /s/ along with the vowel, which results in [ɛhpéd], [ɛhtár], and [ɛhkí]. The latter possibility seems particularly perverse to the teacher of English, since he usually can't hear the [h] and thinks that the student has interpreted his instructions to "drop the vowel" as "drop the 's'."

The kinds of phonological interference described above may have a permanent influence on the recipient language. Phonemes may be added to the recipient language or they may be lost. The phonetic quality of allophones may change considerably. The changes may affect only the dialects of the language in contact with the donor language or they may affect all dialects of the language. The English phoneme /ʒ/ was probably added as a result of the contact with French. Standard Indian English phonetic qualities differ to a significant extent from the phonetic qualities of the model from which it developed, perhaps as a result of interference from the Indian languages which were in contact with the model. In order for such kinds of interference to have a permanent effect, however, they must be accepted by a significant body of the speech community.

MORPHOLOGICAL AND GRAMMATICAL INTERFERENCE

The recipient language in a bilingual situation is subject to *morphological and grammatical interference* as well as to phonological interference. Grammatical interference, when it occurs as a result of the learning of the recipient language, usually has little permanent effect on the recipient language. At least grammatical interference phenomena do not penetrate widely into the written language. If a Mexican student says *I like a lot the new house* when he is learning English, it is unlikely that this instance of interference will lead to the dropping of the normal English syntactic arrangement. [10] The teacher of English as a foreign language should find it useful to become acquainted with the forms of grammatical interference which occur in bilingual communities, so that he can predict the kinds of errors his students are likely to commit in the classroom, especially if he has to write materials to teach English. Grammatical interference is treated systematically in several contrastive studies and will not be discussed here.

LEXICAL INTERFERENCE

Lexical interference is extremely common in bilingual communities and items resulting from lexical interference are often integrated into the recipient language. When the lexical items become integrated, they no longer provide occasions for interference, [11] and are called *loans* or *borrowings*. An examination of the kinds of lexical interference may give the teacher of English an idea of the linguistic forces at work when student errors occur.

On the basis of the extent of substitution, Haugen distinguishes all lexical borrowings as either *loanwords* or *loanshifts*. Loanwords import all or a part of the phonemic shapes of their models, but loanshifts do not. [12] A *pure loanword* imports the phonemic shape of the model completely. Examples of pure loanwords in Puerto Rican Spanish are *Mr., teenager, party,* and *beauty parlor.* The closeness of phonemic resemblance to the model depends partly on the proficiency of the speaker in the donor language, and partly on how well the loanword is integrated. [13] Complete substitution of recipient language phonemes for those of the donor language takes place in the speech of monolinguals in the bilingual community and when the loan has been completely integrated. Monolingual speakers of Puerto Rican Spanish pronounce *teenager* as [tínayel] and *Mr.* as [místel] ([l] is often used instead of [r] in syllable-final position in Puerto Rican Spanish). The Hungarian form of *tease* /bɔ́ssantaʃ-/ is used by some Hungarian-English bilinguals in Montreal in otherwise English contexts such as /-ʃiz-bɔ́ssan-taʃiŋmì/ *she's teasing me.* The loan retains its Hungarian phonemes, presumably because it has not yet been integrated into the Hungarian English of Montreal. A *loanblend* imports part of the phonemic shape from the donor language and substitutes recipient language morphemes for the rest of the item. Haugen gives as an example of Pennsylvania German *blaumepai,* where *pai* is imported from English, while the German form *blaum* is substituted for English *plum.*[14]

Loanshifts are called *extensions* or *creations.*[15] Loanshift extensions add donor language meanings to words which already existed in the recipient language. Loanshift creations import the morpheme arrangements from the donor language, but use recipient language morphemes. Loanshift extensions may be *homophonous,* i.e., only the sound has influenced the adoption of a new meaning. Haugen cites as an example American Portuguese *grosseria,* "a rude remark," which developed the extended meaning "grocery." Loanshift extensions may also be *synonymous.* Although there is no similarity in sound, there is a partially overlapping semantic range. Greater overlap results from the importation of a meaning into the recipient language. Haugen gives the American Portuguese word *frio,* "cold weather," which has imported the English meaning "infection." If the loanword resembles the model both phonologically and semantically, the loanshift extension is *homologous.* Canadian French has added the meaning "baby carriage" to *carrosse,* "coach." Loanshift creations may have a morphemic composition which corresponds exactly to that of the donor language, as in Canadian French *être dans le même bateau,* "to be in the same boat." These are also called loan translations. If the loanshift creation changes the morphemic composition, as in Canadian French *selon l'angle avec lequel nous regardons* from English "depending on the way you look at it," it is known as a *loan rendition.*

The teacher of English as a foreign language who knows the native language of his students and the kinds of lexical borrowings described above will be able to recognize a host of errors that might otherwise go unperceived. Many errors of this type fall into the category of false or partially false cognates. For instance, the Spanish student says in English, *I passed the exam* when he means that he took the exam. Since *I passed the exam* is an acceptable sentence in English, the teacher may let the remark pass, unless the context will not permit the normal English meaning. However, lexical interference may be more complicated. A French Canadian student of English once said to me at the beginning of a conversation *I threw myself into the fire yesterday* when he meant *I got into trouble yesterday*. He was modeling his English sentence on the Canadian French loan rendition *se jeter dans le feu,* which is probably based on the English expression *out of the frying pan and into the fire*. The teacher of English can write vocabulary lessons organized on the basis of the kinds of lexical interference which take place in bilingual communities since the same kinds of interference also occur in the English class. He can thus help to prevent some of the vocabulary problems that are likely to arise.

Interference always occurs in bilingual communities. Linguists have stated that the structural differences between the languages in contact can explain most specific cases of interference. [16] Linguists rate bilingual proficiency on the basis of the amounts of interference that an individual demonstrates in his use of each language. A "perfect" bilingual would be someone who showed no interference in either language. Although linguists are particularly interested in ascribing interference phenomena to the differences in the structures of the two languages in contact, they realize that psychological and sociocultural factors must be considered, too. Not all differences in the structures of the two languages actually cause interference. For example, the French and English pronominal systems differ considerably in form and distribution. Frenchmen learning English seldom experience difficulty with English pronominal patterns, although English speakers have considerable difficulty learning the French patterns. (This probably has something to do with the greater complexity of the French system — and the development of relative scales of complexity as a device to help predict interference in cases such as this is an interesting possibility.) Not all bilinguals in a given bilingual situation experience the same problems of interference. Structural differences cannot explain why interference results in lasting changes in one of the languages and not in the other. Psychologically and sociologically oriented investigations of bilingual individuals and bilingual communities have offered other explanations for interference phenomena as well as other insights into bilingualism. These are of concern to linguists and teachers of English alike who may refer to the studies edited by Rice and Osgood and Sebeok for an introduction to these aspects of bilingualism. [17]

[1] Leonard Bloomfield, *Language* (New York: Holt, Rinehart and Winston, 1933), p. 56.

[2] Einar Haugen, *The Norwegian Language in America* (Philadelphia, Pennsylvania: University of Pennsylvania Press, 1953), Vol. I, p. 7.

[3] Einar Haugen, *Bilingualism in the Americas: A Bibliography and Research Guide* (Publications of the American Dialect Society, No. 26, 1956), p. 9.

[4] Uriel Weinreich, *Languages in Contact* (New York: Publications of the Linguistic Circle of New York, No. 1, 1953), p. 1.

[5] See, for example, Haugen, *The Norwegian Language in America, op.cit.* pp. 370 ff.

[6] For examples of structural changes in both languages, see M. B. Emeneau, "Bilingualism and Structural Borrowing," *Proceedings of the American Philosophical Society,* CVI (1962), pp. 430-442.

[7] Haugen, *Bilingualism in the Americas, op.cit.,* pp. 39-41.

[8] William G. Moulton, "Toward a Classification of Pronunciation Errors," *Modern Language Journal,* XLVI (1962).

[9] Weinreich, *op.cit.,* p. 18.

[10] See Weinreich, *op.cit.,* pp. 39-46 for instances of grammatical integration.

[11] Haugen, *Bilingualism in the Americas, op.cit.,* p. 41.

[12] Haugen, *The Norwegian Language in America, op.cit.,* p. 391.

[13] Haugen, *Bilingualism in the Americas, op.cit.,* pp. 55-56.

[14] Haugen, *The Norwegian Language in America, op.cit.,* p. 390.

[15] *Ibid.,* pp. 400-404.

[16] Weinreich, *op.cit.,* p. 3.

[17] R. A. Rice, (ed.), *Study of the Role of Second Languages in Asia, Africa, and Latin America* (Washington, D. C.: Center for Applied Linguistics, 1962).

C. E. Osgood and T. A. Sebeok, (eds.), "Psycholinguistics: A Survey of Theory and Research," *Journal of Abnormal and Social Psychology,* Supplement to XLIX (1954).

IV

TEACHING CLASSICAL LANGUAGES: THE STRUCTURAL APPROACH

C. Douglas Ellis

WHY "CLASSICAL" LANGUAGES?

The discipline known as modern linguistics may seem by its very name to exclude, at least by implication, a good deal of the traditional kind of language study commonly carried on in our schools and colleges. Textbooks in linguistics often appear to take an unusual approach to language and, for those new to the field, they certainly introduce a number of unfamiliar terms. If this is the case with linguistics generally, the area known as applied linguistics will, for many readers, seem more esoteric still. The name may recall accounts of intensive language courses, research into exotic languages taught in neither school nor college, perhaps even suggest the exciting possibilities of machine translation and, for some, point to the endless vista of studies in communication. Since, however, the field of applied linguistics is so deeply involved with the most recent advances in theory and technique, the question may well be raised: "Why include in this volume a chapter on classical languages and the structural approach (a development within the field of applied linguistics) — or, for that matter, on classical languages at all?"

By way of an answer let us say right away that the proper field of linguistic science is the study of human language in all its forms and of the ways in which it is related to other kinds of human activity. Classical languages are as much forms of human language as any modern tongue. What is more, many people are deeply interested in acquiring a mastery of one or another of the world's classical languages. If linguistic study can help us in this task — and it is often an exacting one — then it is important to learn what linguistics has to say in this connection.

The formal study of language has traditionally been a time-consuming task. This is even more so in the case of classical languages. Today, many students feel uneasy about devoting a major part of their time and effort to the study of an "ancient" language in the face of more immediate pressures. This uneasiness or reluctance is sometimes experienced in spite of considerable interest in classical studies for themselves and an awareness of their contributory value in the pursuit of humane studies generally. As a result, the place of the classical languages in today's crammed curriculum has come in for searching reappraisal, especially in Europe and North America. One suspects that similar pressures are gathering force in other parts of the world as well. This is reflected not merely in the adjustment of secondary school programs to meet more immediate needs, but also in the modification or abandonment in recent years of the "Latin requirement" for admission to most major universities in the Western world, or for the obtaining of the Bachelor's degree.

When all the foregoing has been said, it is still generally conceded that a student of any modern literature with roots in the past, or of comparative literature, of history, linguistics, law, philosophy, religion, and a variety of related disciplines, has a signal advantage if he can read primary sources in the relevant, classical tongue. This is to say nothing of the intrinsically valuable educational experience of studying classical antiquity, whether it be of China in the T'ang Dynasty, Japan in the Heian Period,[1] or of classical Greece and Rome. Whatever the case, if classical studies are not to continue their gradual decline and ultimate disappearance except from the study of the specialist, something other than a holding action must be undertaken. While there appears to be widespread agreement in this respect, the same degree of concurrence is not always present in proposals as to the precise measures to be adopted. Insofar as the languages themselves are concerned, certain useful principles and constructive steps may be outlined, derived though they may be from a discipline which is, properly speaking, outside the range of classical studies as such.

Foremost among the goals to be reached are the reduction of unacceptable time requirements in language learning and the boosting of teaching and learning effectiveness. An effort to achieve these aims and counteract some of the pressures mentioned has resulted in a move to adapt the techniques of modern applied linguistics to the teaching of non-spoken languages.[2] The method, based on a structural analysis of both the language to be taught, commonly called the "target" language, and of the learner's native language, referred to as the "source" language, is known as the *structural approach*. In cases where the analyses have been good and the method properly applied, results have been gratifying and provide ample justification for using the methods of applied linguistics in the teaching of classical languages as well as of those spoken today.

The structural approach is based on the view that language is a set of *learned behaviour habits* — a code involving signal units in certain permitted patterns. While the capacity for using language is genetically transmitted, the specific language which a speaker controls is acquired through a process of social conditioning. In other words, language has to be learned. To be used effectively, moreover, it has to be learned so that one can produce the required grammatical and sound patterns without having to stop and think at every step. Control of the language patterns has to become a matter of habit, and this is what we have in mind when we describe language as one of the sets of behaviour patterns which go to make up the folkways, or culture, of a given community. If a language is to be used easily and effectively, the patterns must be grooved in until they become habitual responses. The value of such reflex conditioning is, after all, that it avoids wasteful duplication of effort. Any activity carried out repeatedly in a set of circumstances similar to that in which it first occurred will be less likely to need working out step by step each time it is performed. Instead, it can be based on a familiar pattern of stimulus and response with minor adjustments to fit the immediate situation. Nativelike command of a language is the ability to make just such responses to given stimuli, automatically *and correctly:* i.e., not to have to "work out" every construction like a piece of algebra.

In the preparation of language learning material it has been noted that the first step is to make or obtain a careful analysis of the language to be studied and of the learner's own tongue. Attention to the learner's own language may seem an odd proviso until one reflects on the commonplace that "languages *are* different." It is precisely the kinds of difference between languages which give rise to the troubles experienced by the learner. In both cases one must discover the signal units at the various levels of structure (i.e., phonemes, morphemes and the various syntactic units. Cf. Chapter II.) and their patterns of organization. It is only after one recognizes these units and their distinctive types of combination that it becomes possible to produce the kind of drills which will drive home new and different contrastive patterns. The next step is to build the carefully programmed drills themselves. In these the student is conditioned to respond appropriately to given stimuli: to recognize contrasts which are new to him and to disregard others which, although operative in his own language, have no significance in the language which he is learning. What gives a language its unique identity, after all, is not just a different set of words, but a structural mechanism all its own, not quite like that of any other language. The behaviour habits of a speech community are different from those of every other speech community and learning a new language involves learning new cultural perspectives at the linguistic level.

In the structural approach, the careful control and gradual buildup of steps by which the new language code is taught ordinarily results in the student's losing less time than under traditional teaching programs, or even under an approach such as the so-called "direct method"[3] (sometimes confused with the structural approach). Emphasis is placed on acquiring a control of the structural mechanism of the language, and from the outset the student learns to handle this deftly and correctly. In short, he "learns the grammar" in the truest sense of the word as contrasted with "learning *about* the grammar,"[4] a goal often receiving greater emphasis under a more conventional system.

As the student proceeds in his carefully programmed approach, drills are supplemented with shorter, then gradually longer segments of reading material followed by questions controlled to elicit specific responses (in the target language). Meanwhile the student is developing progressively greater sensitivity to structural stimuli and, while lexical understanding is still limited, structural understanding should be much increased. The experience of the learner at this stage has been compared with that of the native speaker who reads unfamiliar, technical material in his own language for the first time. He ordinarily recognizes verbs, nouns, or adjectives, in the sense that he understands the construction of the passage even though he is unsure of the precise dictionary meaning of some of the terms. After practising a sequence of carefully designed drills, such as those described above, reading in the target language now becomes an exercise much more like reading in the mother tongue. Of course the student consults a dictionary for new words; but since he ordinarily recognizes what kind of new word it is (verb, noun, etc.), i.e., has structural understanding, this operation now becomes much more like using a dictionary in his own language. He understands the basic thrust of the passage. It is only the referential content of the new lexical item which he has to look up. The situation is rather different — even the reverse — of common experience in Latin and doubtless other classical languages as well.

Where the initial stages of such a program are carefully planned and conscientiously followed through, the student develops a facility in handling the structural signals and learns to read — and think — *in the language which he is learning.*

At this point a word might be said regarding the "direct method"[5] mentioned above. This method consists essentially of confronting the student with the target language alone from the first moment of instruction. New materials are taught through context of situation. Pictorial illustrations and other devices developed through the inventiveness of the teacher, reinforce the linguistic context. The approach is necessarily inductive. Texts are usually programmed cumulatively, and a system of this sort exhibits certain advantages as well as certain drawbacks. Among the former may be listed the constant presence of a native speaker (at least under ideal conditions) as a model for mimicry, and the continued stimulus to communicate in the target language only. Among the shortcomings should be noted the frequent lack of pattern-drill materials and the equally marked absence of adequate descriptive statements. (When this occurs at the phonological level it constitutes a particularly serious lack in a spoken-language course, even where the native speaker is on hand as a model.) In the teaching of classical languages, where a native speaker is by definition inaccessible,[6] the absence of the latter two features may form a serious drawback indeed. An ancient alphabet, after all, represents once existent sound targets; and where these were different from those of the source language in question, some satisfactory and reasonably consistent mode of realizing them must be achieved. Where circumstance further restricts the use of the language almost exclusively to the reading-writing level, there is a normal tendency to focus on translation. The resultant, and inevitable, reduction of ability to function freely within the target language alone can be counteracted effectively only by adequate drill materials designed to groove in the pattern of the code. These in turn should be supplemented by descriptive statements based on a careful structural analysis. In this way the student learns to control the code on the one hand, and on the other, to recognize at the level of conscious awareness the distinctive units and their patterns of combination at every level.

LANGUAGES ARE DIFFERENT.

We noted earlier that languages are different. This is true from the level of sound-system all the way up through the various levels of grammar. For example, most describing words in English and other Indo-European languages are classed as "adjectives":[7] e.g., "big", as in the sentence, *The book is big.* In Algonquian languages, spoken in Canada and the United States, most describing words fall into the stemclass called "verbs": e.g., *mišaaw* — "it is big." The sentence given above, if translated into Cree, a widely spoken Algonquian language of Canada, would be: *Mišaaw masinahikan.* This could be roughly paraphrased as, "The book bigs." The intransitive verb, *mišaaw,* can change its inflexional suffixes to show many different grammatical categories: person and number of subject, order, tense, mode and submode — things which an Indo-European adjective never does. When a clear-cut description of the structural characteristics of each language is provided, the points of difficulty in learning can be plotted with considerable accuracy.[8]

In general it may be said that any two languages will exhibit certain features in sound systems, grammar or both which are fairly similar. Other features will be markedly dissimilar, and a third group will be somewhere in between. For teaching purposes, these areas which display different degrees of difficulty should be marked out and taught through specially devised drills. As a rule little trouble is caused by closely similar features, and only slightly more with strikingly different ones. Their very difference makes them easier to remember. (To transfer association of the describing function from adjective-type words, as in English or French, to intransitive verbs, as in Cree, is really quite a change but one which is quickly grasped by most students.) It is on the middle ground, where things sometimes look partially the same and partially different, that the main troubles usually occur — and this for understandable reasons. A feature which is quite unlike anything in the learner's own language will, by virtue of its dissimilarity, stand out all the more. It may be difficult for the student to produce at first, but at least he can recognize it. At the level of phonology, features which occur in both languages but fulfill a very different function in the two codes are much harder to master. A quick look at the distinctive /k/ sound (or phoneme) in English and the nearest, corresponding sounds in two other languages will illustrate the point.

If an English-speaking student experiments with the following series of words:

kill	: :	skill
cull	: :	skull
called	: :	scald

he will notice several interesting sound patterns.

After all the /k/ sounds in the left-hand column, there is a brief puff of air released before the ensuing vowel is pronounced. After each of the /k/ sounds on the right-hand column there is no corresponding puff of air or, at least, it is not as marked. Obviously there are in English two noticeably different types of /k/ sound preceding the vowel nucleus of one-syllable words: one with a puff of air, or "aspiration," released after it and one with no such puff of air. Wherever the /k/ is preceded by an /s/ the puff of air will disappear. Yet until this difference is drawn to the attention of a native speaker of English he usually fails to note its existence. Even after noting it, he still feels these are just two ways of making the "same sound," and as far as the sound system of English is concerned he is quite right.

If the native speaker of English now repeats the words again, working down the left-hand column, he will note a change in the point of contact between the tongue and the roof of the mouth as he makes the initial /k/ sound. From *kill* to *called*, the point of contact moves farther back along the palate. Working down the parallel column the same thing holds true from *skill* to *scald*. Two patterns now emerge: the difference in production of the /k/ from left to right-hand column being the disappearance of the aspiration; the difference from top to bottom row being the movement backwards of the position of articulation as the adjacent vowel is farther back. We have now listed six perceptibly different types of /k/ sound in English. They can be phonetically transcribed as they occur in our list of words in the following chart:

$$[\underset{\wedge}{k}^h] \quad : : \quad [\underset{\wedge}{k}]$$
$$[\hat{k}^h] \quad : : \quad [\hat{k}]$$
$$[\underset{.}{k}^h] \quad : : \quad [\underset{.}{k}]$$

The important thing to note here is that *they are all accepted as varieties of the same, basic sound signal in English*. The variation among them is conditioned by where they occur in the stream of speech and by the surrounding sound material. No native speaker of English ever uses these differences to distinguish between words which are in other respects the same.

Now let us look at Urdu. Here we find a shift between a [k̂] made at the front of the palate and a [ḳ] made farther back, very much as in English. Both belong to a single sound unit, /k/, and the adjacent sound material conditions which variety of the /k/ signal is produced. In the matter of aspiration, however, following the stop in initial position, the case is very different. Unlike his English counterpart, the Urdu speaker uses the difference to keep otherwise identical utterances apart:[9]

/kal/ - "famine" : : /k^hal/ - "skin"
/kãsi/ - "bronze" : : /k^hãsi/ - "cough"
/kona/ - "corner" : : /k^hona/ - "to lose"

Obviously the speaker of English, when learning Urdu, must become aware that a difference which in his own language has no signaling value now becomes important as a contrastive signal. Moreover, since he has been conditioned in his use of English to pay no attention to this difference, he must now become sensitive to its role in Urdu and react to it accordingly. Language learning involves learning to *make new distinctions* which are significant and to *overlook old distinctions* which carry no significance in the new code. This new point of view, since it affects a set of culturally conditioned behaviour habits, amounts to the achieving of what we have described as a new "cultural perspective".

In Arabic, the English-speaking learner will need to note the difference between a backed and fronted "k"-type sound, and respond differently to each. Both types exist in English but never function as contrastive signals. In Arabic, on the other hand, /ḵalb/ with a fronted production of the initial consonant means "heart," and /ḳalb/, with the initial stop produced further back along the velar surface means "dog." The Arabic-speaking student of English must learn to treat both types of the voiceless, dorso-velar stop as variants of the same signal which, of course, they are — for the native speaker of English. With the development of new cultural perspectives there must emerge new behaviour patterns to match.

The kinds of distinctions illustrated above are found in many different languages and with many different series of consonants.[10] For example, a three-way contrast existed for stop-consonants in Greek of the Classical period:

	I		II		III	
phatós φατός	— "utterable"	*pátos* πατος	— "path"	*bátos* βάτος	—	"bramble- bush"
theós θεός	— "god"	*teós* τεος	— "thy": (poetic)	*déos* δέος	—	"fear"
géras γέρας	— "gift of honour"	*kéras* κέρας	— "horn"	*khéras* χέρας	—	"hands": (poetic)

An effective way of teaching new contrasts is through the use of *across-and-down* drills: down the columns to learn each separate feature and across the rows to drive the contrast home. A drill of this kind may embody eight or ten items in each column. This allows the student ample opportunity to practise careful mimicry either using a tape recording or following a teacher.

A language such as Latin does not appear at first sight to confront the student with many serious problems at the level of the sound system. Two reasons probably account for this: the phonology itself is relatively uncomplicated and, in the absence of native speakers, each major language group has developed its own graphophonic parallels.[11] The second of these two statements simply means that various groups have developed conventional sound values for the written symbols, producing in this way a series of spoken signals which more or less parallel the contrastive patterns represented by the graphic units. In doing so, however, each group (whatever its background language) often intrudes a liberal amount of its own sound system into what it calls Latin. Naturally, then, Latin becomes quite easy to pronounce. In fact, however, a great many of the fairly well attested phonetic characteristics of Latin phonemes (and those of classical Greek as well) are quietly discarded for the sake of convenience.[12] As a result, scholars from different native language backgrounds, able to handle Latin textual materials with ease, have often been baffled by each other's spoken Latin.

As one might suspect, it is not only phonetic characteristics which are disregarded, but even phonemically contrastive features may be overlooked.[13] Vowel length in Latin is a case in point. Most readers of Latin distinguish between the length of the penultimate syllable of *dūcere* on the one hand and that of *tenēre* on the other. Unless, however, the context is poetic, few bother to mark the difference between *nŏvī* and *nōvī, lăbor* and *lābor, mălum* and *mālum*; and, as far as English speaking readers are concerned, the distinction between *erō* and *errō, calidus* and *callidus*, is commonly observed in the breach. Yet much of the attractive quality of Latin verse and, a good deal of prose too, resides precisely in the artistic effect achieved by a control of certain patterns of phonemic arrangement. In verse, rhythm is syllable-timed, with the fall of predictable stress either reinforcing the meter or running counter to it to produce a stumbling, samba-like effect. The situation in English is very different. In most if not all dialects, vowel length is nonphonemic,[14] whereas stress is phonemic. [15] Hence it becomes particularly easy for the English reader of Latin to practise his favourite distortion by substituting stress for length. As a working compromise, we are usually willing to allow the student to treat the Latin and English sound systems as partially the same; but he must also be sensitized to areas where they are unequivocally different. This is best done at an early stage through contrastive drills, as illustrated above. The columns in such drills should list items exhibiting a common feature (e.g., length of vowel, double or single consonant) and each row represents the contrast or contrasts to be learned. The following sample sequence is to lead the student to distinguish between /ă/ and /ā/.[16]

alās — "you may nourish"	ālās — "wings"
labor — "work"	lābor — "I am slipping"
latus — "side"	lātus — "broad"
malum — "bad"	mālum — "apple"
malō — "for a bad" man or thing	mālō — "I prefer"
manibus — "with the hands"	mānibus — "for the shades of the departed"
canī — "for the dog"	cānī — "white"

The matter of graphophonic parallels was observed previously. It should be noted that in certain cases the spoken signal used to represent or realize the written symbol is the result of highly arbitrary agreement. This is very much the case with classical Chinese, where reading convention varies in conformity with the form of modern Chinese spoken by the scholar in question (or his teacher). [17] Where the source language of the teacher is something other than Chinese, any pattern drills devised at the phonological level would reflect the usage of a particular modern speech community. At the grammatical level, drills would be based on the various construction types, grooving these in until they became for the student, a matter of automatic response to given stimuli.

Now to return to the differences between Latin and English. These two systems operate very differently not only at the level of sound system, but at the level of grammar as well.

A common impression made on English-speaking readers of Medieval Latin is that much of it is "easier to understand" than material of classical authorship. The English language relies largely on *word-order* to signal which word goes with which in a construction. Latin does this through *word-form*: i.e., grammatical inflexion. Many medieval writers reflect in their Latinity the influence of their own background vernaculars in which grammatical inflexion was disappearing and in which word order was becoming correspondingly more important. When writing in Latin, they naturally retain the standard inflexional features, but word order becomes much more regularized. As a result, the English reader can in some cases almost disregard features of inflexion (or word form) and depend on a set of word order signals, not unlike those in his own language, to signal constructional relationships. [18] Hence much of the impression of "easiness." Classical Latin does not work this way. Here word order has a function and a value sharply different from anything the student is used to in English. Syntactic linkage is signalled largely through word form — inflexion. The student must be sensitized to the signals peculiar to the Latin code through a series of pattern drills designed to condition him in two directions: (1) not to look for the same information from word order as he received in his own language; and (2) to pick up much of this kind of information from the shape of the words. The student then practises the drills until he reacts on cue, not merely correctly but automatically both in recognition and production. The consequent proliferation of pattern drills is one of the most conspicuous features of a structurally oriented text. Once the constructions to be learned have been introduced, through a block of basic sentences or other basic material to be overlearned by sheer mimicry and memory work, the student is ready to begin drill sessions where he gains practice in the three operations fundamental to the control of any language code: substitution, expansion and transformation of set frames. Translation exercises are curiously absent. Constant insistence on translation, so common in the introductory stages of conventional language learning, can actually militate against the student's feeling at ease with a new set of language habits: i.e., constructions, since every time the new habit is presented the older and more familiar one is promptly recalled as well.

Vocabulary — and it must be learned — is taught in context so that structural as well as lexical meaning is made apparent. The acquisition of lexical items is further promoted through the recognition and production of synonyms (through drills), and the observation of resemblances to English derivatives (conveniently incorporated in a list after the drill section of the lesson). No use remains for the traditional vocabulary section with right and left hand columns to be covered (and peeked at). The word list (if any) in each lesson is relegated to the end, and is for reference and discussion only. All new words have already been learned by the student before he reaches that final section of the lesson.

A further note on drills: these can often take the form of question and answer in the target language — a device equally useful for testing comprehension of the substantive content of a passage or, where tightly controlled, of the grammatical features. Reading passages, verse selections in particular, can be supplied with a (prose) paraphrase in the target language. This technique is used in a widely known text for teaching Latin by the structural approach. [19] In the paraphrase the student often finds the clarification which helps him discover the meaning of the original without recourse to English.

Some day, perhaps, it may become routine, in preparing a language-learning text for class use, to see language for what it is: one of the sets of learned behaviour habits that goes to make up a total culture. In the case of a classical language this would suggest taking a series of typical, cultural situations from the period represented by the literary corpus and presenting them through blocks of carefully selected literary material. Around each of these nuclei could then be developed a language-learning unit based on the best insights of modern, applied linguistics. Other levels of the classical culture in question would then be taught simultaneously with the language. If a program of this nature were thoughtfully worked out there is no reason why, at the end of his first year's study, the student should not achieve as good a control of the classical language as he would of any modern language similarly taught. Certainly he should experience much more reward in using a language with a certain sureness of give and take, rather than engaging in an exercise more reminiscent of fitting together the pieces of an exacting jigsaw puzzle. The end result, in short, should not be to convince the student that the language he is trying to learn could never possibly have been spoken naturally, by real people, but rather to leave him with a sense of freedom, even enjoyment, in handling the new code, and a consequent liberty to center his attention on the subject matter in hand.

---

[1]The comparison was suggested by Professor P. T. K. Lin of the Department of History, McGill University, who pointed out, however, that these centuries were not the most productive in philosophical inquiry although they represent an era of considerable literary activity.

[2]Waldo E. Sweet, *Latin: A Structural Approach* (Ann Arbor: University of Michigan, 1957), is the outstanding example of this sort of material for speakers of English. A second and more fully developed version is *Latin: Level I,* by the same author, published by Encyclopedia Britannica Films, Inc., 1966.

[3]For the "direct method", cf.n. 5. It should be emphasized that since it is the structural mechanism of a language and not just or even primarily a different lexical inventory which gives it its peculiar identity, in structurally designed materials, vocabulary may be limited to well under a thousand words. There will, however, be a heavy concentration on the structural patterns. Once the structural features of the code can be handled with ease, the student can readily build in new vocabulary as required.

[4]To be able to handle the language well is to know the grammar. To teach a control of the basic patterns is precisely the aim of the pattern drills. The inductive approach leads from the actual language behaviour to the rules which describe it. In this way the student learns the grammatical description by reflection. The grammar itself he has already learned from the drills.

[5]Perhaps the best known use of the "direct method" is in the widely popularized Berlitz system. Direct method materials for the teaching of Latin are C. W. E. Peckett and A. R. Munday, *Principia* (Shrewsbury: Wilding and Son, Ltd., 1949), and a sequel by the same authors and publisher, *Pseudolus Noster,* (3d. ed., 1959). Of interest also is William G. Most, *Latin by the Natural Method* (Chicago: Henry Regnery Co., 1957, 1958, 1960), 2 vols. Cf. also D. Lepoutre, "Relatio Experimenti Cujusdam," *Vita Latina,* No. 23, Dec. 1964, pp. 101-105; also letter of S. Bails, *Vita Latina,* No. 20, Nov. 1963, p. 121; Cf. also *"Quomodo nonnulli scholastici Lugdunenses ad Latine loquendum sonoris cellulis usi sint",* Madeleine Bonjour, *Vita Latina,* No. 27, April 1966, p. 22; *"Une expérience d'enseignement du latin au laboratoire de langues",* G. Hentz, *Vita Latina,* No. 27, April 1966, p. 30.

[6]With the exotic exception, of course, of persons deliberately shielded from learning the language of the larger community and brought up to use a classical language in the home. There are also others who speak Latin or Sanskrit, for example, but who learned it as a second language.

[7] Adjectives are, properly speaking, a grammatically defined class of words: i.e., (in English) they display certain paradigmatic features and may occur in certain syntactic positions. Many words indicating qualities or attributes (e.g., *goodness, greed*) are not adjectives. The Latin term, *adjectīvus,* signified a word added or applied to another. Obviously the *grammatical* behaviour of "adjectives" is not the same thing in both languages. The fact that they describe qualities or attributes is of interest, but not a diagnostic feature of the stem class. When one meets a describing word in Algonquian, which patterns grammatically in the same way as all intransitive verbs in the language (e.g., "he blushed"), the mere fact that it describes does not justify calling it an adjective. In Cree, nearly all "describing" words which match English adjectives are intransitive verbs. To call them "adjective verbs," as has sometimes been done, is to introduce a double confusion: the confounding of grammatical classes in the first place and the mixing of grammatical and semantic principles of classification in the second.

[8] Cf. Robert Lado, *Linguistics Across Cultures* (Ann Arbor: University of Michigan, 1957), p. 2 ff. This study is addressed primarily to the trained teacher of foreign languages and provides useful guidance in locating points of difficulty for language students.

[9] The examples were kindly supplied by Professor M. A. R. Barker of the Islamic Institute of McGill University, from his text, *Spoken Urdu,* 1967.

[10] e.g., voiced, voiceless, post-aspirated, glottalized, etc.

[11] The term was suggested to me by Professor M. L. Kay of the Department of Languages and Linguistics, York University, Toronto, in a discussion on a workable pronunciation for a course in classical Greek.

[12] For an account of these, the well-known studies of Roland G. Kent, *The Sounds of Latin;* Edgar H. Sturtevant, *The Pronunciation of Greek and Latin;* C. D. Buck, *Comparative Grammar of Greek and Latin;* W. M. Lindsay, *The Latin Language;* and more recently, L. R. Palmer, *The Latin Language* and W. S. Allen, *Vox Latina* should be consulted.

[13] The disregard may take the form not only of overlooking a distinction in the system, but of deliberately skewing the vocal signal represented in writing in conformity with the practice related to an alien but more familiar spelling system: e.g., where Latin "c" is sometimes realized vocally by the English-speaking reader as [k], and at other times by [s], usually before front vowels.

[14] The analysis represented in Trager and Smith's *Outline of English Structure* is the one followed here.

[15] In Latin, of course, the situation is the reverse: vowel (and consonant) length is phonemic, whereas, if the rule of Ennius is observed, stress is phonologically predictable (and hence nonphonemic).

[16] Cf. W. E. Sweet, *op.cit.,* pp. 5 and 6 for drills in sound contrasts.

[17] I am indebted to Professor M. L. Kay for alerting me to this situation.

[18] Due attention must also be given to the fact that this increases the redundancy of signal tremendously, thereby further facilitating comprehension.

[19] W. E. Sweet, *op.cit.*

V TEACHING AND TRAINING: BRITISH EXPERIENCE

A.V.P. Elliott

Languages have been taught, or at least learned, in Europe for centuries. Latin was taught in the schools from early times and Shakespeare suggests that French was learned at least by royal personages in England. Later, well-bred young ladies learned it as an "accomplishment." But it is only comparatively recently that modern languages have been taken seriously in Britain; some might even complain that they are not taken seriously today. Certainly modern language teaching has been unduly influenced by traditions and fashions. The old grammar and translation approach is still to be found; elsewhere there are various practices going under the name of "direct method"; while the term "mental discipline" has found its way into at least one fairly recent government pamphlet on the subject.

But when the teaching of English began in parts of what was then the British Empire, it had at least the opportunity of a fresh start. The opportunity was not always taken. Up to twenty years ago, the "grammar grind" was still to be found in some schools in East Africa. Back in the nineteenth century, Macaulay hoped that the study of English would do for India what the Classics had done for Europe. Some would argue that India has never recovered from this unfortunate start.

But there were others who later on took the opportunity of making a fresh beginning. One of these was Dr. Michael West. At about the time of World War I he was working in what was then India, now East Pakistan. It seemed to him that in the schools in his area, the senior pupils needed to learn to *read* English, though they would never have to speak it. He accordingly devised a series of school books which aimed at teaching English through reading, and at developing the reading ability of the pupils. (The word "student," in British use, is confined to those receiving higher education.) West's books were based on the principles of "vocabulary selection," first developed by Thorndike in the United States, and of the introduction of a few new words at a time, and their frequent use immediately after their first introduction. The books were known as the *New Method Readers.* They were later used in Africa and eventually all over the world, adapted to the needs of those who had to learn to speak English as well as to read it. West wrote a number of other books and many articles. He was also largely responsible for the "General Service List of English Words" which is an authoritative work on word frequency in English. West is undoubtedly one of the great names in the short history of our subject.

The period between the wars was one of growth and development in English teaching, both in Africa and in the Far East. In Africa, the growing need for English-speaking civil servants stimulated the work in schools. The publication of new and better school books, like those of West, helped to guide both expatriate and local teachers into better methods of teaching English. There was much speculation on the function of language in African development. A number of pamphlets issued by the British Colonial Office of the period display a kind of linguistic schizophrenia. There was undoubtedly a need for English in Africa. But the German scholar, Westermann, whose influence was considerable, turned people's attention to the African languages and to the importance of a child's mother tongue in his education. There were also semi-mystical ideas about a people's language being "its soul."

In Japan the growing interest in English led to the appointment of Harold Palmer as adviser on English teaching and later as head of the English Institute in Tokyo, where he was joined by A. S. Hornby. What they did for the teaching of English in Japan is now perhaps little understood, for much of it disappeared into the tragedy of World War II. But for the war, there is no doubt that Japan would now be a shining example as far as English studies are concerned.

Hornby continued the work in Japan until the war and then joined the British Council. It was in this capacity that he became the founder and first editor of *English Language Teaching,* a periodical now known all over the world. He also published many works over the years, and has been particularly successful in advising teachers of English both in person and through his publications.

Palmer continued his studies after his return from Japan. His understanding of the problems of language teaching was profound, and he gained considerable insight into the nature and working of language at a time when the study of general linguistics was less known and less developed than it is today. At least one worker in the field of language teaching suspects that Harold Palmer foresaw most of the developments we are familiar with today. If West and Hornby were the high priests of the movement, Palmer was certainly its prophet.

Other influences began to make themselves felt. At the University of London Institute of Education, Dr. (later Professor) P. Gurrey began to interest himself in the problems of teaching English overseas. British teachers, destined for work overseas, began to follow courses at the Institute and came under his influence; and later on teachers from overseas countries were also sent to London. After World War II the work in English as a second language was expanded, and a full department started, by Professor Bruce Pattison. Over the years, the Institute has had a marked effect on overseas education in general, and on the teaching of English in particular.

The end of World War II, and the movements towards independence, further stimulated the development and improvement of English teaching in the Empire — soon to become the Commonwealth. Ghana, the first African country to become independent, adopted English as the language of administration. There, as in other African countries, the need for English speaking teachers, administrators, technicians, and diplomats became acute.

In the East, the movement for a national language accompanied independence. The government of India was anxious that Hindi should eventually be adopted for this purpose. But Hindi has not been popular in southern India, and English remains to some extent a lingua franca and as a second language to be taught in schools. In Ceylon, Singhalese became the national language, and in Malaysia, Malay. The difficulty of getting minorities to accept a language not their own remains acute, though English seems to have an undiminished popularity. In Indonesia, the use of Dutch was discouraged after independence, and a national language was instituted. English became the first foreign language to be learned in schools.

An important postwar development was the gradual concentration of the British Council's resources on English teaching. The Council had been founded between the wars as a means of spreading British cultural influence. Its activities were manifold — literary, artistic, musical, among others; perhaps they were too amorphous to be always effective. Not infrequently the Council's knuckles were smartly rapped by the Press. But in the promotion of English teaching the Council found something which it was well suited to do. Through its agencies and officials abroad, and especially through its language officers, it has stimulated the teaching of English by advice, libraries, teaching, lectures, refresher courses, and the like. It has also brought numbers of teachers to Britain for further training, in English teaching and in other subjects; and it is a channel through which many British people find their way to English teaching posts abroad. Its activities have extended to the teaching of English to students from overseas in London and to the housing and development of the English Teaching Information Centre (ETIC) with its excellent library and other valuable activities.

This development was largely in response to the first Commonwealth Education Conference which met at Makerere University College in Uganda in 1961, and its successor in New Delhi in 1962. The latter was particularly concerned with the supply and training of teachers of English as a second language; with the exchange and dissemination of information on the teaching of English; and with the use of English in the Commonwealth. In many countries there was (and is) a shortage of teachers competent to teach English at different levels, and still more, a shortage of well qualified people to staff the teacher training instititutions on which, ultimately, the quality of English teaching depends.

One development which may point the way to better teaching in several parts of the world was the foundation at Allahabad,

India, of an English Language Teaching Institute, financed by the Nuffield Foundation and by the government of the Indian state in which it is situated, Uttar Pradesh. Another Institute, the Central Institute of English, was later set up at Hyderabad, financed in this case by the Ford Foundation. Officers of the British Council, as well as staff recruited through the Council, and Indian specialists, teach in these centers, which are mainly concerned with teacher training but which also arrange in-service courses for teachers.

Mention should also be made of the contribution of Australian and New Zealand specialists to English teaching in Southeast Asia, New Guinea, and the Pacific area. In Australia, the University of Sydney is responsible for a course in the teaching of English as a second language and the Commonwealth Office of Education has been active in preparing TESL materials, as well as in research on TESL methodology. In New Zealand an English Language Institute was established in 1961 at Victoria University, Wellington.

This survey should not end without reference to the contribution of Canada to the teaching of English abroad, through her many teachers who serve abroad for several years as part of the CUSO and the External Aid programs of that country.

Few would nowadays deny the importance of adequate training for teachers of languages, or indeed of any subject. Yet not so long ago, it was believed in some quarters that anyone who spoke English or French or German as his native language would be quite competent to teach it to foreigners. Through English schools there flitted a succession of "monsieur"'s, "herr"'s and "mademoiselle"'s, all notoriously (or fictionally?) bad at keeping order, but all, it was thought, necessary to the proper teaching of French and German. Even today, persons concerned with education in distant parts of the globe lament the fact that there are so few English men and women available to teach English.

But times have changed. No one who knows anything about language teaching would now maintain that it is *de rigueur* to have a native speaker in a school to teach his own language. Better, most of us would maintain, to have a well trained local teacher, than a native speaker with no training at all.

To speak of training teachers of language implies four questions: *who? when? how long?* and *what?*

Who, then, should be trained as language teachers? First and foremost, those who already have a good command of the language in the four basic skills — understanding, speaking, reading, and writing. Alternatively, those who are likely to acquire a good command of the language with further instruction.

It must be explained here that, in Britain and in countries influenced by British practice, two kinds of training are known. First, there is the one-year course in a university department of education which is normally taken immediately after graduation. Secondly, there is the "training college," now known in Britain as a "college of education," where students remain for anything from two to four years, continuing their education, including language learning, and receiving professional training.

Language teachers should be fully qualified professional people. Sometimes they will teach more than one language, or even more than one subject. But they should essentially be *teachers,* taking a broad view of their subject, and not mere technicians.

When should people be trained to teach language? British experience suggests either after a degree course (in the relevant language), or after school is ended at eighteen, in a college of education. But in other countries where British influence has affected the educational system, training takes place at various levels,

How long should a course last? This depends very much on local circumstances. For those who already have a command of the language, two years is possibly ideal. In practice it is more often a matter of one year in Britain for teachers of English abroad since grants to both British students and overseas visitors are seldom given for more than a year. In Asia and Africa, where teachers of English are frequently trained in the "training college" type of institution, further instruction in English merges into methodology, and it is difficult to say how much time is actually given to professional topics.

Finally, the question *what?* What should be the content of a training course? Whatever else is done, it is certain that two, and sometimes three, subjects must form the backbone of such a course.

These are, first, teaching about the language, its phonology, its grammatical structure, lexis, and verb system. This is, in fact, linguistics, but linguistic theory applied to the language in question. General linguistics has, in the writer's view, little to contribute to a teacher's course, except in a very simple form, as an introduction, and, if there is time, at the end, in order to widen the students' view of the subject. It should also be noted that, since language teachers have to teach both form and function, the semantic issues cannot be avoided.

Secondly, there is the methodology of the subject. Students learn what is involved in teaching the language in a particular kind of school and to pupils of a particular age range. They learn the various techniques of teaching the language, including the making of simple aids, and the handling of mechanical aids. They also have periods of time teaching in schools under supervision.

Thirdly, for students in "training colleges" there must be further teaching of the language itself. Where non-native speakers are involved, too, special help may be needed in such matters as fluent speech and reading ability, both vital factors in a future teacher's life and work. In some places, perhaps more especially in a university course, work should be done on the literature of the relevant language, on the various uses to which the language is put, and on the dialects and registers which are characteristic of certain places and of people's work and speech.

TRAINING IN BRITAIN

Mention has already been made of the University of London Institute of Education and its long connection with English as a foreign language. (Other universities use the terms "second language" or "English overseas.") There are now a number of other colleges and universities in Britain which are concerned with this work at various levels.

A total of ten courses is run at the University of Bangor (Wales), Leeds, London, Manchester, at the College of Advanced Technology, Cardiff (which has university status), and at Moray House College of Education in Edinburgh. No two of these courses are exactly similar.

One of the two courses at Bangor is called the "Postgraduate Diploma in English as a Second Language." It is conducted by the Department of Linguistics, and is largely linguistic in content though there is a section on principles of second language teaching. Bangor's other course is called the "Diploma in Education with special reference to the Teaching of English as a Second Language." It also is for graduates, and is conducted by the staffs of the departments of Education and Linguistics. The explanation of this apparent dichotomy is that there is a need for the further training both of experienced language teachers and of young graduates who are starting their teaching careers. This distinction is also made by Leeds University, where there is a "Postgraduate Diploma in English as a Second Language" for young British graduates, and a course in the teaching of English as a second language for qualified persons from overseas. In London, where both courses are held in the Institute of Education, there is a Diploma course for qualified and experienced teachers of whom the majority comes from overseas, and a Certificate course for young British graduates. Courses of this kind at London, Leeds and Bangor include work in educational studies so that students may obtain their first teaching qualification as well as training for work overseas.

The course at Manchester University leads to a "Diploma in the Teaching of English Overseas." It is for overseas and British students, and both graduates and qualified nongraduates are accepted. The College of Advanced Technology at Cardiff has a Diploma course (in the teaching of English as a "foreign language") for qualified and experienced graduates. At Moray House, Edinburgh, on the other hand, we are simply told that students "are drawn from many parts of the Commonwealth" for the Diploma course, and likewise for the Certificate course, which is directed more to the primary school situation.

All these courses last for one academic year which in Britain is normally from October to June inclusive.

The content of these courses does not differ widely, except that the courses for young British graduates contain educational studies. They all include linguistics in some form. Sometimes it is described as "General Linguistics," and is accompanied by work on the "structure of English" (Bangor) or "English grammar" (Leeds). In London, linguistic theory is directly applied to English, and in the Moray House courses it does not appear under this name at all. Most of the courses include "phonetics" or "phonology" as well as work in the methodology of the subject. Leeds and London include some work on the teaching of literature and London pays some attention to the spoken English and the reading ability of its overseas students.

The overseas students attending these courses come from all over the world and include, as is natural, a large number from Commonwealth countries. Some arrive through the agency of the British Council, others are sent by their own governments or come as private students. In programs like the London Diploma course, or the Manchester course, the range of educational background and of ability is very great. Graduates with good Honours degrees rub shoulders with students who have nongraduate teaching qualifications. The latter sometimes prove to be the better teachers, though they may find the academic work, especially in linguistics, very difficult.

Students on some of the courses teach under supervision for part of the year. In February and March the British graduates of London and Leeds work in Spanish schools; the London Diploma students go to Malta in the second part of their course; and some students teach immigrant and other children in Britain. The importance attached to work of this kind differs from university to university and from course to course.

At the end of June, when the academic year finishes, most of the students take an examination. The overseas students then return to their countries while the British graduates are put in touch with posts abroad by the British Council or other agencies.

In addition to the programs described, there are a number of universities in Britain offering work in linguistics and phonetics. In two cases such courses are related to language teaching. The one at Edinburgh in applied linguistics is intended for senior persons who are concerned with language teaching; the University of Essex offers a course in applied linguistics leading to the Master's degree. At other universities, too, advanced students are studying or writing theses for higher degrees. In London, where the Master's degree in Education is now by examination, some of the ablest students in the Diploma course stay on an extra full year to follow a special course in linguistics, literature and the teaching of English as a foreign language and are thereafter examined for the M.A.

There is no doubt that these courses are having and have had considerable influence on the teaching of English in many places abroad. Students who have attended them go home and spread the new ideas and techniques they have learned in Britain. University teachers and others concerned with teaching English visit other countries where they are able to influence the work and to derive knowledge about the background from which their students come.

Much depends upon the status of those who apply for entry to university departments in Britain. Inspectors, teacher trainers, and the like can exercise considerable influence when they return home. The influence of ordinary teachers is considerably less. British universities can, certainly, accept or reject those who apply to them; they cannot guarantee that all who apply are in influential positions. In practice a number of teachers are brought over to Britain, often for reasons which are not purely academic. These are sometimes at the mercy of bad syllabuses, textbooks, and examinations when they return home. They learn modern English in Britain only to find that local examiners still insist on the application of outworn grammatical "rules." Some give up the struggle, and return to their former ways of teaching, thus wasting the large sums of money spent on their year in Britain. Others soldier bravely on, sometimes earning the disapproval of inspectors and others in authority.

This gloomy picture is not however true of all places. There is no doubt that training in Britain is having a very considerable influence on the teaching of English in Africa, the Middle East, the Far East and elsewhere.

This chapter is concerned mainly with the teaching of English, but we must not forget that teachers of other European languages are being trained in Britain, mainly in university schools of education.

Teachers of English, and of other languages, are being trained in many, if not all, countries. In Africa and Asia, such training varies widely. On the one hand there are some highly efficient training centers, like the English Institutes in India and certain university departments and training colleges in Africa. But there are still far too many ill-equipped and poorly staffed colleges where little more is attempted than the improvement of the student's own English. The effect of this dubious kind of enterprise is to turn the colleges into poor imitations of secondary schools. Often the students in such places are those who have failed to enter either secondary schools or some center of higher education. Sometimes methodology is taught, and teaching practice undertaken. Where this happens, teachers are at least being trained for their future work, and the results may be very encouraging. No work which could be called linguistics is usually undertaken in training colleges, either because there is no one to teach it, or because the students have not enough English or previous education to grasp the essentials of the subject. Students coming to Britain from overseas countries often find linguistics difficult, even when its principles are directly applied to a language of which they have some knowledge. Many such students have been taught a smattering of traditional grammar, and find it difficult to comprehend new concepts.

There is obviously great need for improvement in the training of language teachers in some places. This makes it all the more desirable for those who staff the colleges abroad to receive further help and instruction in Britain and other countries.

EXAMINATIONS AND TESTS

In Britain public examinations of an academic kind are organized by the universities. Sometimes a number of universities form a group for this purpose; or a single university like Cambridge may run its own examinations. These examinations are at two levels. Pupils take a number of subjects at "O" (ordinary) level, at the age of sixteen; and they take one, two, or three subjects at the advanced or "A" level at the age of eighteen.

With the development of education in places like Africa, Malaysia and the Caribbean, Cambridge and London began to make their school examinations available to pupils overseas. (London has gone further and awarded external degrees. There are many proud graduates of this university who have never been within a thousand miles of it.) In a good many places abroad, Cambridge "O" and "A" level examinations are taken. These are modified for the overseas customer but the standard is said to be equivalent to the home product; for this reason, and because of the name of Cambridge, the examinations are extremely popular. There is no doubt that they have exercised a beneficial influence on school work and on education generally.

For some time past people connected with language teaching have interested themselves in a more scientific kind of test than conventional examinations provide. Educational psychologists and statisticians have done a great deal of experimental testing and have provided the statistical tools for the job. During World War II, John B. Carroll, a well-known psychologist with considerable understanding of language, worked out a number of tests to discover military personnel with an aptitude for learning foreign languages, like Japanese. He worked on the assumption that certain types of performance in the mother tongue, such as the discrimination of speech sounds, would be a guide to foreign language learning ability. He also took his subjects through the early stages of a specially invented language. The work was experimental and is described and assessed in *Training and Research in Education* (Pittsburgh: University of Pittsburgh Press, 1962).

On the British side, a certain amount of work done during the last twenty years has been set forth in the journal *English Language Teaching,* (XV, 1). P. Strevens describes the work done at the Phonetics Department, University of the Gold Coast (now Ghana) sixteen years ago to develop an oral English test for West Africa. This was intended to replace a conventional test which was based on reading aloud and conversation. The test which was devised consisted of three parts — reading, comprehension, and conversation. The reading test contained certain known difficulties in the country concerned. The examiner had a list of these and marked the candidate's performance accordingly. The comprehension questions dealt with general understanding and with specific points in English phonology and grammar. In the conversation test, the examiner chose a subject and marked the candidate's responses for fluency, accuracy and good vocabulary.

Another number of the same journal (VII, 2) contains a long article on achievement tests by D.F. Anderson who, after teaching English abroad, returned to the University of London to work on testing. Anderson was concerned to improve examinations by making them more objective and his article contains strong criticism of existing examinations used overseas. He described a test which includes the understanding of spoken English, the understanding of written English, expression in writing, and expression in speech. Whether Anderson's tests were ever used abroad is not known since he departed to other work — a misfortune for the field of language teaching and for testing in particular.

The whole question of examinations in English was investigated by the Commonwealth Educational Liaison Committee which was set up by the first Commonwealth Conference at Makerere. They restated the distinction between objective and nonobjective tests, that is to say between the testing of pinpointed details and the general examination of the Cambridge type.

An objective language test may for example test the candidates' ability to discriminate between two vowel sounds. On the candidates' paper there are two words, *sit* and *seat*. The examiner says *sit*. The candidates underline the word they think he said. Another example might be the testing of their ability to use question tags. On the candidates' paper is printed;

> *It was awfully cold yesterday, . . .*

followed by three "tags":

> . . . *isn't it?*
> . . . *wasn't it?*
> . . . *was it?*

They are required to underline the tag they think is correct.

Such questions, said the Commonwealth committee, are easy to mark but difficult to set; whereas the nonobjective kind of test is easy to set ("Write a short essay on . . .") but difficult to mark in the sense that if three examiners mark an essay, their marks can easily be widely different.

The committee also set out the areas which can be tested, namely phonology, grammar, lexis, orthography and the combination of all these skills in the production and comprehension of larger chunks of spoken and written language. These tests may be based on the target language itself or, some would say, on the results of contrastive analysis of the target language and the mother tongue. The committee concluded that in the early stages of language learning objective tests are appropriate, since anything the pupil produces, spoken or written, will be either right or wrong; but that in the later stages, when pupils have some flexibility in the use of the language, nonobjective tests should be used. This is a common sense conclusion, but it is still desirable for the nonobjective tests or examinations to be based on modern methods of teaching and modern techniques of testing.

Examinations, the Commonwealth committee pointed out, have a great influence on teaching programs and methods. (Many years ago in England intelligence tests were introduced as one means of determining which kind of secondary school eleven-year-olds should go to. The primary schools then started training their pupils in doing intelligence tests!) The conservatism of examiners has often held back the development of a modern approach to the whole business of language teaching. So far only *achievement* tests have been discussed, the business of assessing how much a pupil has learned, whether he has learned it correctly and in acceptable form, and whether he is worthy to be awarded this or that certificate or other piece of paper.

Other kinds of test are the prediction test, such as Carroll's tests referred to above, aptitude tests, to find out if candidates' command of a language is sufficient for this or that purpose, and diagnostic tests, which might be used to discover special difficulties and their cause.

An experimental *aptitude* test was worked out between 1963 and 1965 at the University of Birmingham, England, by Dr. Alan Davies, now of the University of Edinburgh. The purpose of this test was to assess the aptitude of persons overseas for further study in the United Kingdom. British Council officers and others are frequently asked to assess such persons' English, and the test was set up, validated and standardised to help them in their task. It included tests of phonemic discrimination, comprehension of phonological and grammatical items, reading speed, and the comprehension of reading material as applied to either science or arts subjects.

A great many more experiments in language testing have been carried out than can be mentioned here. The subject is by no means closed and there is still much work to be done. The techniques of testing need to be spread to places where they are still largely unknown or at least not applied to language work. In particular there is a need for those concerned with nonobjective examining to know something of achievement testing and perhaps to modify their examinations accordingly.

In a chapter largely concerned with Britain and the Commonwealth, mention must be made at this point of an American, Robert Lado. His work on language testing is well known and his book on the subject (*Language Testing,* London: Longmans, Green & Co., Ltd., 1961) is a standard work. If it is not yet known all over the world where English is taught, it certainly deserves to be.

TESL AND THE MIGRANT

In the past, the great migrations of people have been from east to west, like the voluntary migration of Europeans and the forced migration of Africans to America.

Since World War II, migration has restarted on a larger scale. The disturbances caused by the war in Europe and the separation of many from their homes produced great numbers of displaced persons who were ready to seek a new life in the comparatively empty lands.

Australia has taken large numbers of Europeans and, as far as the English language is concerned, has organised a number of courses through the Commonwealth Office of Education. Migrants took their first course at the port of embarkation in Europe; this was called a "pre-embarkation" course. Then there was further teaching of English on the voyage, and for this a textbook was devised called *English on the Way.* The voyage from Europe to Australia takes a month, and during this time a certain amount of language teaching can be accomplished. W. F. Mackey, who has had experience of shipboard teaching both on the Australian run and on the much shorter Atlantic crossing to Canada, describes the problems and the techniques in an article in *English Language Teaching* (XI, 3). Shipboard teaching is rather like radio teaching. You cannot be sure of your audience, for individuals may well be absent from the lessons because of other attractions, because of seasickness, or for other reasons. Constant repetition is therefore necessary, and the use of audio-visual media is desirable, especially films or film loops which hold learners' attention better than anything else. The amount which can be taught is limited, but the material can be reinforced by a textbook, by oral practice and by group practice.

On arrival in Australia the migrants were sent to reception centers where the English teaching continued; finally, they were allotted to districts, occupations, and homes in the Australian community. At this stage they were taught more English through evening classes, correspondence lessons, and radio lessons. The book used for these purposes is the now well known *English for Newcomers to Australia* published by the Commonwealth Office of Education.

All this work has gone through several phases. Shipboard teaching was at one time abandoned, but was reintroduced after 1955. The radio lessons began in 1949, and the correspondence course in 1950. In 1963 the two were combined into a radio correspondence course. *English for Newcomers* in its modern form is based on structure grading, on oral practice and on the development of aural-oral skills before reading and writing.

Australia clearly faced the migrant problem systematically. The teaching of English is only one part of the work. Houses had to be built, reception centers organised, jobs found. Among other kinds of training is a special radio course for new Australian women, called "Making Friends." And the existing population had to be prepared for the inrush of newcomers.

Since the war another migration has been taking place across the Atlantic to Canada. Immigration into Canada is controlled by the federal government, but there is no federal office of education, as there is in Australia. Education is a matter for each province, hence it falls to the provinces and particularly to Ontario, which receives most of the newcomers, to organise the teaching of English for them. This has been done mainly through night schools which are staffed by professional teachers who work during the day in public or high schools, though there has also been a number of volunteers from outside the profession.

The general pattern of immigration into Canada is that the migrants land at Montreal or Halifax and make their way, many of them to Ontario, where there are jobs in commerce and industry. A few go immediately to Quebec or the Maritimes, to the prairie provinces, or to British Columbia; others drift West later on. Recently arrived migrants tend to form themselves into unified ethnic groups, living together like the Italians in Toronto or the Ukrainians farther west. Later generations are sometimes more dispersed and are absorbed into the English-speaking or French-speaking communities.

The training of teachers of English to new Canadians has also been carried out provincially. In British Columbia, teacher training has been undertaken at the University of British Columbia summer session, while Ontario has for the past nine years organised an excellent summer school for these teachers in Toronto. Acting on the principle that teacher training must always be accompanied by teaching practice, they have run concurrently a night school for Toronto immigrants. Those who have worked at the Toronto summer school have a vivid recollection of hot summer evenings when several thousand new Canadians crowded in to learn more English.

At the beginning, the textbook for English teaching was *Learning the English Language* which had been prepared at Harvard and which consisted largely of Basic English. Later, a series of books based on modern linguistic principles, and called *Let's Speak English* were written by Professors Robinson, Theall, and Wevers of the University of Toronto and published by W. J. Gage. A further course was written by Carson W. Martin, and published by the Department of the Provincial Secretary and Citizenship, Ontario.

There has always been migration to Britain (as well as from Britain). Small groups of people, Flemish weavers, Huguenots, French aristocrats, Americans, Australians, Hungarians, and others have from time to time made their homes in Britain. Until recently there were no barriers, and Commonwealth citizens could come and go freely. In the dock towns of Liverpool and Cardiff there were West Africans, Arabs, and Chinese. And in the Soho quarter of London dwelt a motley collection of Italians, French, Germans, Greeks, and others.

But in Britain as elsewhere, the big migrations started after World War II. First tne West Indians, then the Maltese and Cypriots, then the Indians and Pakistanis flooded the country until the government was forced to pass the Commonwealth Immigration Act to halt the flow, or at least to reduce it.

Immigrants to Australia and Canada are mostly European and skilled. Immigrants to Britain are largely non-European and mostly unskilled. In many cases they were needed. Indeed some firms started or increased the flow by inviting them. But in general they were not needed for skilled jobs. There are now, of course, a number of them and their children who have been trained to skilled work — doctors, nurses, bus drivers, technicians, and so on. But since they were not initially required for skilled work, there was not the same pressure to teach English to the adults.

It was in the schools that the pressure was felt. In certain districts of London, in Birmingham, the northern cities and anywhere where work was to be found, the schools found themselves with forty, fifty, sixty percent of immigrant children. None of the teachers had any experience in teaching English as a second language. The children were from many linguistic backgrounds. The West Indian children spoke English as their mother tongue, but their dialect was unfamiliar and sometimes unintelligible to the teachers who spoke and were accustomed to one of the various British dialects. It was the moment for a great national effort in language teaching.

What actually occurred was local, piecemeal, and haphazard. Some local education authorities — the Inner London authority, for example — faced the difficulty squarely and began to organise short courses for teachers who were trying to teach English to the newcomers. Some help was given by university departments concerned with teaching English overseas. The teachers themselves formed an association which has done first-rate work in training and assisting its members.

The problem is intensified by the fact that children are normally drafted into the schools at the age of five or on arrival in Britain. Once in the schools, teachers are unwilling to segregate them from the British children for more than part of the time. Thus immigrants are taken out of the regular classes for their special English periods and then taken back for other work. There is much talk of "integration," meaning the stage when immigrants know enough English to do all their work with the other children. In a few places immigrant children are sent to special centers to learn English before entering the ordinary schools. This seems to be a better arrangement.

The great need is for teachers who understand the principles of teaching English as a second language. In addition to those following the short courses organised by the local authorities, a few teachers are attending university courses aimed chiefly at teaching English overseas. Such persons should be able to help other teachers later on.

Several schemes of research have been planned on the immigrant problem, both sociological and linguistic. The University of Leeds has work in hand on linguistic problems, while London has a pilot scheme of investigation into the English an immigrant child will require to follow secondary school work.

The main problem, however, is a continuing one: How to teach the immigrant child enough English for him to benefit from his education according to his standard of ability.

THE OUTLOOK

Robert Lado's book *Language Teaching* (New York: McGraw-Hill, 1964) is subtitled "A Scientific Approach." There is or can be a scientific approach to many activities not in themselves scientific. There is a scientific approach to cooking, to painting, and to producing a TV program. The question is whether one needs to understand the science in order to perform the activity. The science behind language teaching may be in the description of the language by a trained linguist, and in his contrastive analysis of the language with the mother tongue of the learners. The machines, like language laboratories, which aid language learning are the products of modern science. A teacher uses the machines; he may teach the language according to some description of it and perhaps according to the results of contrastive analysis. But must he understand the science to perform the activity? Must the car owner understand everything under the hood before he drives the vehicle?

A British writer is likely to be sceptical about these matters, though it must at once be said that there are those in Britain who, influenced by American thinking, believe that linguistics is the be-all and end-all of language teaching.

British work on foreign language teaching has been largely empirical. West in India assessed a local situation and prepared his textbooks to meet it. The work of Palmer and Hornby was initially based on conditions in Japan. Others attempted to meet the needs of Africa. In all these places English was a school subject, taught by professional teachers. Their training may have been weak or nonexistent, but they believed in their subject. As education developed, English became the medium of instruction above a certain level; and for those who were sufficiently able, it was and is studied up to university standard.

Of course theories existed. West developed vocabulary selection which Thorndike had initiated. Later on, when the importance of structure was realised, experiments were carried out in the grading of structure and in the writing of books based on this work. At Cambridge, Ogden and Richards developed *Basic English* as the practical result of scholarly speculation.

After World War II interest in linguistics developed in Britain. Many of the linguistic theories were of transatlantic origin, though it must be observed that J.R. Firth, first Professor of Linguistics in London, had been working on the subject for some time, as had other scholars in different parts of Europe. There are now a half dozen departments of linguistics in the country outside of London, while at London University there are people concerned with linguistics in several contexts. What effect are these departments likely to have on language teaching at home and abroad? One effect they are having is to make linguistics better known. As it becomes better known a certain orthodoxy develops among some of the disciples and there are those who believe that linguistics is all in all to language teaching. Others are more sceptical while retaining their interest in the subject. It is true, they would admit, that linguistics has done and can do much to make teachers aware of the intricacies of language. It can also provide them with a new model of the language they have to teach. But which model? Fashions of linguistic analysis succeed one another with some rapidity. Is it to be immediate constituent analysis, or generative and transformational grammar, or the kind of grammar being worked out by Professor Halliday in London, or an amalgam of all of them?

Has linguistics anything to say about the *methods* of teaching second languages? Many linguists recommend pattern practice as described in Robert Lado's book. But surely this is based on psychological rather than linguistic principles. What has psychology to say about language teaching? Probably a great deal, though much needs to be written for the benefit of language teachers. One of the most important books to appear recently on this subject was Wilga M. Rivers's book *The Psychologist and the Foreign Language Teacher* (Chicago: Chicago University Press, 1964).

We speak of "applied linguistics," but what is linguistics applied to? The description of the language to be taught, the equipment of the teacher, or the methods of teaching?

Such questions are subjects for speculation and discussion among thoughtful teachers in Britain and in places where British teachers are working.

Contrastive analysis was a device originally worked out and applied in the United States. There are those in Britain who believe that it is a desirable preliminary to language teaching in a particular area. Others are most doubtful. Are all mistakes, they ask, due to mother-tongue interference? Will not the teacher soon become aware of his pupils' difficulties anyway? And there is of course the purely practical problem of analysing so many languages in the parts of the world with which Britain is concerned.

There is continuing thought and discussion about the methods of language teaching. Pattern practice may have its place, but it is not enough. At some stages pupils must learn to use the language in contexts of situation, otherwise they will never be able to use it outside the classroom.

Then there are the machines. Generally speaking — and it is a broad generalisation — British people take less readily to gadgets than do Americans. Language laboratories are used in many schools and colleges in Britain, but their use is limited and experimental. They have their place, like the blackboard, but they cannot replace the teacher. The same is often said of teaching machines. We are not anxious to replace the teacher, as some claim the machine threatens to do, for we believe that education is primarily a matter of human contacts, and language learning is part of education. Language laboratories are fashionable just now, but overseas it has sometimes been necessary to discourage authorities from buying them because of the absence of both technicians to mend them and competent people to programme them. Radio and television, however, are quite widely used both in this country and overseas. The BBC have been teaching English by radio ever since World War II, and have more recently turned their attention to television. Most of their work has been aimed at individual adult learners, but inevitably their programs have also been used in schools abroad. A large number of radio programs for various levels of learner has been broadcast in Europe and elsewhere, and many of these are available on records. One television series for beginners and for more advanced learners has been made, and in conjunction with the British Council, the BBC have produced two series of films designed to help teachers of English abroad, called "View and Teach."

One of the greatest uses of such programs, as of records and tape, is to enable people overseas to hear native English voices. This is important both in language teaching and in the teaching of literature at a higher level.

While all these things have their uses, it must be remembered that many schools abroad where English is taught have neither television nor radio receivers, nor indeed electricity. It is hardly surprising that the subject of electronic devices is a somewhat academic one for persons who teach in such places.

Second language learning is a school subject, taught by professional teachers. The question therefore arises, what is the new language to be used for? Reference has already been made to the use of English as the medium of instruction in a number of places in Africa and in the East. One reason for this is the bewildering number of African languages, many of them spoken by comparatively few people, or even lacking a written form, with the consequent absence of textbooks. Another is that representatives of several languages may often be found in an African classroom. In the East, where language communities are larger, English is not the medium until the university. All this raises a number of problems. In Africa, many pupils learn through English before they really know enough English. In some eastern countries, owing to the low standard of English in the schools, it is necessary to have preuniversity classes to teach students enough English to enable them to follow university courses.

In countries where education is far from universal and where there is fierce competition to reach the higher classes, there is the problem of those who leave school after two or four years of English. Should the early English lessons be aimed at teaching simple, accurate English to early leavers? Or should the aim be to lay foundations for those few who will have a full school course? Experienced language teachers know fairly well what ought to be done, but local teachers are sometimes too weak in their own English and have too little training to do anything but follow an indifferent textbook.

But there are those who, in Africa and Asia as well as elsewhere, manage to reach the top of the educational ladder. They have achieved a good command of English; what are they to do with it? The whole question of advanced work in English is relevant to them, and many teachers are concerned with this. So much work has been done on the sheer mechanics of learning a second language, too little on what comes later. For some pupils, and for some university students, English literature is important, and a number of people are interested in the difficult task of presenting it to learners who have never seen Britain or any other country where English is the mother tongue. Others must be concerned with science and technology and a number of English texts have been produced by British writers to prepare these learners for the textbooks which they must eventually read. In university courses abroad some students work on contemporary English from both the linguistic and the literary points of view. This work is promising and is worthy of further development.

Because of all this, many British and Commonwealth teachers are concerned with the whole language, and not just with the initial stages of teaching it to those who did not know it. In the present and future practice of second language teaching, certain vital questions need to be asked, though they cannot all be answered in full.

The first of these questions is: Is second language learning to be for the few or for the many? In Britain today, education is being influenced by egalitarian doctrines. One result is that experiments are being made with the teaching of French in primary schools. A more immediate reason for this, according to some, is that children should learn spoken French before they meet the more rigorous discipline of the grammar school. There are arguments for and against these experiments, of course, but the notion that everyone should learn a second language is not confined to Britain. Overseas, people learn English as a second language if they move far enough up the educational ladder. How much English, depends on how long they stay at school. For a long time there has been, in many countries, only one kind of secondary education, but as distinctions develop between academic, technical, or other kinds of school, the question of second language teaching for all secondary pupils will have to be answered. It should be answered on the basis of the number of teachers available, and on their knowledge of English and their training. The number of competent teachers of English at present available in Africa and Asia suggests that English should be severely restricted. On the other hand, English is the known road to a good job; and it is undoubtedly desirable that many kinds of people should understand, speak, read, and write it.

The second question is: Should one new language be taught in a country, or two, or three? In some of the African countries where French is taught as the second language, English is taught as the third. In Nigeria, French is taught in some schools as the third language. There are good political, commercial and diplomatic reasons for this, but it is a strain on a country's educational resources. There is the question of Latin. This is no longer an essential in British schools, but Africans sometimes wonder why it has been denied to them. In Britain, pupils learn French as the first foreign language and German or Spanish or Russian later on, according to their choice. But need everyone learn the same languages? At present English is considered important in Africa and many eastern countries. But the need for other languages will eventually arise, and it might then be a matter of one pupil learning language A, another language B, and a third language C.

The third vital question is: What *kind* of language should be taught? Ought everyone to learn to understand, speak, read and write? Or could some specialise, say, in reading? When we look round at the languages being taught in the world today, especially English, we have to recognise the fact that spoken language — as one might hear it in the streets of Moscow, Paris, London, or New York — is not taught. A brief comparison of a transcription of speech and a language textbook will soon convince the reader of this. Most language teachers believe that oral work comes first. Most teachers will soon insist on *he's coming* rather than *he is coming*. But their first priority is to teach the use of the essential, basic structure of the language, and this precludes most of what we know as spoken language. It precludes response sentences, for example, those remarks which we use when someone else is speaking, like: *Oh, did you? . . . So did I. . . . You're telling me.* Later on, of course, some of these should be taught. But in the early stages we are much more concerned with getting our pupils to say what is fundamental and typical in the language than what comes naturally to a native speaker.

Because English is a lingua franca in many of the places with which we are concerned, it looks as though many people must learn some kind of spoken English. Professional people must also learn to read, because nearly all the scientific, legal, medical, and other books are in English. But must everyone learn to write? And in particular must they learn to write the sort of English which examiners demand of them?

All over the Commonwealth there is a shortage of teachers. This is partly because of expansion in education, partly because other professions are more attractive and partly because, in Africa, teachers are drawn to posts in the civil and diplomatic services. It seems doubtful whether there will ever be enough teachers in some countries which are too poor to educate many of them or to offer them, when educated, sufficiently attractive conditions. There is also a shortage of adequate teacher training in many countries, partly through misunderstanding of its importance and partly through lack of funds. It is therefore all the more important that teachers should be used economically.

The final question is whether progress in second-language teaching, or deterioration, is likely. We have the knowledge now for efficient language work, but how is it carried out, and how will it be carried out in the future?

Education is often dogged by conservatism, and no subject more than second-language work. So much that has been developed for the teaching of English abroad has hardly touched modern language teaching in Britain. Old-fashioned teaching is also to be found abroad, even in the hands of expatriate teachers who should know better. But apart from teachers' own convictions, often very strongly held, the big need, as has been indicated before, is for efficient teacher-training. Those teachers of English as a second language who are trained in Britain are well trained, because there is the personnel to do the work properly. Overseas it is another story. There is effective training at centres which are few and far between, at the African universities, for example, and at the English Language Centres in India. But there are many teachers of English who have had very little training or none at all. Will the situation improve? The answer must depend on politics and economics, on the will to improve, and on the technical ability to improve. We are concerned with so many places where the political situation is anything but stable. Political disturbances can ruin the best of educational intentions. Likewise there are so many places which are relatively poor in resources and others which are relatively rich, but where the resources have not yet been tapped. The will to improve language teaching depends ultimately on the rulers — both politicians and civil servants. These have to balance educational against other needs and to stretch finance tightly over as much as it will cover. Governments come and go, and are notoriously fickle in their interest in education, medicine, agriculture, arms, community development, and so on. But where there is the will to improve education, something can be done; where there is the will and the means, a great deal can be done. Then it is a question of resisting the claims of those areas which may be called "window-dressing" — elaborate buildings, huge university sites, enormous technical colleges; and of putting the resources into teacher training which may not impress the populace but which underlies all other forms of educational advance. Only thus shall we see real progress in second-language teaching in some Commonwealth countries. It can be done or it can't be done. Which is it to be — progress or deterioration?

VI

TEACHING ENGLISH TO SPEAKERS OF OTHER LANGUAGES

Monika Kehoe

TESOL (Teaching English to speakers of other languages) appears as the title of this chapter because TESOL embraces a wider category of language activities than the more familiar TESL. It is used here to cover problems of the immigrant child and the foreign student *in* North America, as well as those of the teacher *from* North America working overseas.

THE IMMIGRANT CHILD

Immigration officials of underpopulated countries, such as Australia and Canada, have had long experience with the individual who arrives with little or no control of the language of his adopted country.[1] Over the years, many second language programs have been instituted on the migrant's behalf — before his departure, on shipboard, as noted in the previous chapter, and, of course, after his arrival. Because he must know English in order to work, he has a strong incentive to learn, and his association with other English-speaking workers on the job helps him to acquire the fundamental speech patterns of his new tongue in a relatively short time. For his wife and children, without his exposure to and involvement in the second language environment, the new language may be far more difficult to acquire. The children of school age suffer a particularly serious initial handicap as the language barrier isolates them in a kind of limbo of despair.

In those schools where funds are too limited or foreign pupils too few to warrant adding a special ESL teacher, immigrant children are often placed in regular classes where they sit for a while, dazed and uncomprehending, until they become restless and troublesome from the boredom of their solitude. As a result they may develop into serious disciplinary problems or become drop outs, eager to stay home where they are understood, or associate only with those who speak their mother tongue. Because immigrant neighborhoods are so often poor neighborhoods, the schools they support cannot afford to pay for additional specialized staff even when there are enough foreign children to make up a separate class in English. The alternative, should there be one, of transporting the pupils to a center for second language instruction where they can spend all their school time in learning English, is also financially impractical.

Attempts have been made to solve the language problem of the immigrant child by engaging the services of teachers' aides or obtaining the assistance of volunteer groups of women to teach English informally on a part-time basis.[2] The latter plan takes the children out of the classroom for various activities which involve the aural-oral use of English in a natural though limited way. It relieves the teacher of the supervision of these nonparticipating pupils while it allows them to use their school time to make some progress in English, the essential tool of their further education. Although, certainly not an ideal solution, this kind of "live" instruction has important advantages over thrusting the foreign child into a classroom situation where he is certain to feel lost and ignored and where the content of the course he needs most, namely English, is likely to be concerned with literacy or literature rather than with language. (It may also be noted here that this type of voluntary part-time work may involve the college-graduate housewife in stimulating and personally rewarding activity.)

The handicap of being exposed to course material which does not meet his needs, the immigrant child shares, as we shall see later, with the foreign student who enrolls in an English-speaking university or the student learning a second language anywhere in the traditional academic system. The entire question of *literacy* is therefore, of considerable relevance to the success of efforts to teach English overseas as well as at home and perhaps deserves a more detailed examination.

Teaching the "three R's" has for centuries been the concern of the schools, while literacy has served as the line of demarcation separating the "knows" from the "know nots." Traditionally, much of the necessity for literacy stemmed from a need to be able to read the Bible. In the mid-twentieth century, when education is becoming more secularized and less dependent on the printed word, we still rank populations in developing countries by their "literacy rate." We continue to export, with missionary zeal, literacy skills which are today of questionable advantage and efficiency as a method for bringing economically underprivileged peoples abreast of the times. We persist in assuming a pose of shocked disbelief when we learn that such-and-such a country in Africa or Asia has a literacy rate of only 15 percent.

When the articulate inhabitants of the "developing," mainly agricultural, communities protest our insistence on their priority need for literacy skills, we have recourse to such persuasions as that they must be able to read the directions on the bags of imported fertilizer piling up on their wharves under our foreign aid program. When the tribesman wants to know why his wife should learn to write and we reply, "So she can write letters," he is bound to inquire, "Who to?" So sacred is the tradition of the scribe that we continue, even in advanced technological countries, to teach "composition" to countless children who in their adulthood will never write anything more important than a shopping list, and will write that only if their audio-lingual recorders are in need of repair. If this seems a farfetched vision for the year 2000, one need only look back a generation or two to see what miracles science has wrought in the last thirty-five years. In the transistorized society of tomorrow, we must expect at least as much change in communication as we have seen in transportation since Henry Ford put his first Model T on the road.

According to the experts' predictions, reading and writing are likely to become more and more anachronistic forms of communication for the general public as the availability of instantaneous transmission of ideas and information increases. We are told we must anticipate the revolution in education — already underway — that will ultimately result from technological development. We are cautioned not to continue teaching out-

moded skills of a pre-electronic era. Our attention is drawn
to those hours of penmanship practice that the older generation spent when they were in school. The teachers of forty
years ago thought Palmer Method would always be useful — for
writing "letters to friends" — and that typewriters were only
machines for big business and too expensive for an individual
to own. They were wrong. Long-distance telephoning, it is pointed
out, was exclusively reserved in those days for sudden death
announcements or some equally impressive emergency. Now
it is commonly used for casual conversations. There is certainly
some truth in the allegation that the schools are behind the
times, especially in language teaching. So strong has been the
emphasis on the written form of language that until the present century we have hardly paid any attention, even in language research, to the spoken word. Such concern has been
beneath the dignity of scholarship. Writing — "composition" —
has always been the approved goal. With the advent of modern linguistics, we have finally begun to examine living speech as the
important form of language. We have belatedly begun to consider the significance of language as sound. We can be ready, if
we will, to meet the new era of audio-lingual communication.

But the tyranny of literacy prevails in an especially disturbing
way in our secondary schools. There we are not content to
teach reading and writing as tools of access to other subjects,
but we demand of *all* students (immigrants and native born)
a literary standard which in modern society is not only artificial
but impossible for all to attain — anymore than all students
can become artists in any other form, be it music, painting,
or sculpture. We seem to find it difficult to understand the
difference between being able to communicate adequately
and being able to communicate artistically. We spend so much
time on teaching the refinements of composition and the subtleties
of literary appreciation to the untalented and the disinterested
that we become frustrated and discouraged when, in spite of
our efforts, most students do not come up to the standards
of performance we have inherited from the traditional grammar
school. We complain that Johnny not only can't read but he
can't write either. The college blames the secondary school
for his poor preparation, while the secondary school points

to the primary school as the source of the trouble. Reading specialists are called in at the elementary level and more research on reading techniques is undertaken in the graduate school. In between, remedial courses are introduced at the college level where bewildered and embarrassed Johnny is finally exposed to something called "rhetoric & composition" — based on literary models of the written language, including poems and essays of a bygone era — which Johnny hates to learn and his professor hates to teach. These courses, usually concerned more with the mechanics of language than with literature and often labelled "dumbbell English," are geared to failure.

THE FOREIGN STUDENT IN NORTH AMERICA

Often it is into this very same remedial course that the foreign student, handicapped in additional ways, finds himself plunged on his arrival at a North American university. If the course is ineffective for English-speaking students, accustomed to the Anglo-European cultural patterns, how much less effective is it for the foreign students from Asia and Africa who are still reeling under the cultural shock of their jet transition from the vastly different physical, social, and psychological environments of their homelands. Even though they are assigned to a special course designed for foreign students and taught by a trained TESL instructor, they may still have severe difficulty adjusting to the patterns of logic which shape the English language materials they are expected to comprehend or produce.

Few English instructors dealing with foreign students have an appreciation of the tremendous cross-cultural adjustment required of the Asian or African on the North American college campus. The professor supervising the M.A. thesis complains that, unless he rewrites the paper himself, it makes no sense. The organization of the material is somehow just "off." He is dismayed to find that the candidate who speaks good English, has been in North America several years, seems to understand the lectures, and has obviously good control of the spoken language, still cannot develop a logical, written paragraph.

Recognition of the cultural variation in the linguistic backgrounds of foreign students extends far beyond those elements covered by contrastive analysis or comparative stylistics and includes such matters as thought pattern and its development, together with all those psychic factors that Marshall McLuhan illuminates for us so brilliantly in his *Understanding Media*. The linear sequence of thought which print has imposed upon our Western civilization, and which we call logic, is frequently a distortion of consciousness for the Asian or African whose awareness is more a "wrap-around" intuitiveness. The inductive and deductive types of reasoning that shape model English paragraph structure and lead the native reader to expect to find them in formal prose, may be entirely baffling to the foreign student whose mother tongue is an Oriental or African tribal language.

A recent study of "Cultural Thought Patterns in Inter-Cultural Education"[3] describes the paragraph development by parallel construction, common to Semitic languages, and the circular approach by indirection, typical of Chinese or Korean languages. The greater inclination to digress, found in papers of French or Spanish speaking students suggests that even Romance language backgrounds allow much more freedom for introducing extraneous material. The observation that "each language and each culture has a paragraph order unique to itself, and that part of the learning of a particular language is the mastering of its logical system" inevitably leads to the conclusion, too often ignored, that "The foreign student who has mastered the syntax of English may still write a bad paragraph or a bad paper unless he also masters the logic of English."[4] Contrastive rhetoric, as well as contrastive analysis of structure, is an important part of the training of those foreign students from other cultures who are required to write in English at an advanced level.

But the teacher of the ESL course at any level should be aware of the wide cultural gap which exists, particularly for students from Asia and Africa, who must adjust not only to completely different speech patterns but new behavior patterns as well. Differing complexities of social organization and control make for misunderstandings in interpretation and equivalence. English idiom, always difficult for the foreign student, becomes bewildering in the context of strange custom. The teacher who knows, for example, that the Korean language has six styles of address may be somewhat more sympathetic to the Korean student's diffident attitude about greeting anybody and his slowness to adopt the campus formula of "Hi."

The major U.S. universities with large numbers of foreign students from other cultures[5] have attempted to meet some of their adjustment needs with special orientation programs.[6] English second language courses are also provided for those with deficiencies in the basic skills of aural comprehension, oral production (speaking), reading (for speed and comprehension) and composition. Students in these courses are classified according to their results on the English proficiency test which is administered to them either overseas, before their departure from their home country, or at the time of their arrival at the university. When numbers are sufficiently large, they are also grouped by their language backgrounds. This arrangement allows the instructor, who will have some knowledge of the first language of the learners, to focus on the points of interference from their mother tongue. Additional periods in a language laboratory provide the learners with the necessary opportunity for pattern practice drill. Some of the courses are more intensive than others and most are noncredit but required for those students who have failed the preliminary test. Groups are kept small — under twenty, if possible — so that each student may have a chance to speak during the class period.

In those American universities where foreign students are enrolled in the largest numbers, the ESL program is linguistically oriented and the approach is aural-oral with considerable attention given to such frequently neglected matters as intonation. Extensive work in composition is generally reserved for advanced students who need training in thesis writing.

THE ESL TEACHER AT HOME AND ABROAD

Specialist teachers of English as a second language are in demand at many levels both in North America and overseas. They are needed in domestic programs which serve:

1) Adult non-English speaking immigrants who plan to reside permanently in Canada or the U.S. (or in England)

2) Their immigrant children in schools where English is the language of instruction

3) Foreign students (from non-English speaking areas) in colleges and universities

4) North American Indian and Eskimo children

5) Children of culturally deprived groups [7]

6) Civil Service employees (particularly in Canada) or individuals who wish to be bilingual.

They are needed to fill vacancies abroad in education programs sponsored or initiated by:

1) International organizations such as UNESCO or ICAO

2) Government agencies such as External Aid, USAID, USIS, the British Council, the British Ministry of Oversea Education, CUSO, the Peace Corps, Civil Service, Departments of Defense

3) Private organizations such as the Ford or Luce Foundation or private educational institutions such as the American University of Beirut, Pahlavi University in Iran, Robert College, Istanbul

4) Religious and missionary groups such as the Christian Education Movement

5) Individual university contracts such as the Teachers College, Columbia University/London University co-sponsored Teachers for East Africa program; bilateral teacher exchanges under the Fulbright-Hayes Program, the American Council on Education, the Conference Board of Associated Research Councils

6) Private businesses such as the ARAMCO oil company (for example, in their Near East installations), or the ubiquitous Coca Cola Company.

7) Commercial enterprises serving an international clientele, such as airlines, shipping companies, and travel agencies

8) Independent language schools in many countries among which Berlitz is probably the best known.

The list could be extended much further but this will give at least an idea of the breadth of opportunity for TESL specialists. The next question that arises is where can such personnel be trained?

Many universities and colleges in the U.S.A., Canada, and Great Britain[8] now offer courses in the preparation of teachers of English to speakers of other languages (TESOL), or of English as a foreign language (TEFL), or of English as a second language (TESL), as the field is variously called. The TESL, TEFL or TESOL program is so new that it is still finding its place in the organization and administration of institutions of higher education. Sometimes it is part of the English Department and sometimes it is affiliated with the Department of Linguistics or the Faculty of Education. Occasionally, depending on how the university is structured, it is related to all three.[9] UCLA, for example, offers an M.A. in English, Linguistics, or Education with a TESOL concentration. At Columbia University in New York, where there were, in 1966-1967, 120 candidates for advanced degrees in the field, the M.A. is conferred in the Teaching of English as a Foreign Language.

For Canadians, the Laval University program in TESOL has an impressive array of courses leading to both the master's and doctorate degrees. A listing of these indicates how extensive the commitment at Quebec's oldest French university really is. At the same time, it suggests the scope of possibilities in the field for those considering TESL careers: Teaching English as a Second Language, Principles of Language Teaching, History of Language Teaching, Typology of Repetition, Instrumental Didactics, Bilingualism, Preparation of Materials, Analytic Didactics, Organization and Administration of Language Laboratories, Language Teaching Techniques, Measurement of Language Learning: Testing, Audio-Visual Language Teaching, The Teaching of Pronunciation, Language Teaching Practice and Demonstration. Psycholinguistics and Language Learning, General Linguistics, General Phonetics, Diachronic Linguistics, Orthophonic Phonetics, Modern English Grammar, Experimental Phonetics, Descriptive Phonetics of English, The Analysis of Language, Differential Grammar, Comparative Stylistics, History of the English Language, Documentation in Language Didactics.[10]

While highly specialized advanced degrees are available at a number of universities in North America for those with two or three years to devote to higher education, the average language teacher, who may be considering TESL as a career either at home or overseas, can usually give, at most, one summer for retraining in Applied Linguistics. For this purpose, a course in Introduction to General and Applied Linguistics best fulfills the need. Such a course is offered in the summer school or the extension division of a number of universities in the U.S.A. and Canada.[11]

Equipped with at least this minimum introduction to the field, the English teacher with a desire to travel can find a position almost anywhere in the world. Vacancies exist, as has been previously indicated, in United States, Canadian, and British government aid programs which operate in various developing areas of Asia, Africa, the Middle East and Latin America. Inquiries and requests for application forms may be sent directly to the headquarters of these agencies. (See Appendix for addresses.) Besides these, there are the appointments open in private organizations and institutions abroad which are often advertised in the *Linguistic Reporter, Crusade,* or the *Times Educational Supplement.* The last mentioned, and possibly the best source of announcements of TESL vacancies, may carry as many as thirty or forty such ads in one issue. Some of these are for work in advanced nations, it is true, but many of them call to strange, out-of-the-way places. Without doubt, this opportunity for travel and first-hand acquaintance with other countries and other cultures is one of the great (and legitimate) appeals of being a teacher or administrator in a TESL program.

However, for the expatriate teacher in a developing country, there are problems at both the personal and professional levels which make the job more complicated than one of merely improving the language competence of X number of people in Y region.[12] Some of these complications may be indicated by a look at language difficulties in two developing areas.

TESL IN ASIA AND SUB-SAHARA AFRICA
WITH SPECIAL REFERENCE TO KOREA AND ETHIOPIA

The focus of this section will be on two countries, Korea and Ethiopia. They have been chosen for several reasons:

they are areas the writer knows best, second, they present some rather special features in connection with their use of English as a language of wider communication (LWC), and third, because of their relative isolation from the main stream of European influence, they offer clear examples of second language problems which exist in varying degrees throughout most of Asia and Africa.

BACKGROUND

Accidents of geography and history have contributed to make both Korea and Ethiopia almost unique in their seclusion from the forces which, by the end of the nineteenth century, had shaped and modernized many of their neighbors. Korea, "The Hermit Kingdom," was one of the last seclusions in Asia to fall to the blandishments of the West, while Ethiopia, secure behind its highland ramparts, was not "opened up" until the Italian invasion of the World War II. People of both areas resisted the encroachment of outsiders and were suspicious of the motives of any nation attempting to pierce their defenses — social, political, or ideological.

Cultural histories of Korea and Ethiopia detail the many frustrations and misunderstandings responsible for the riddle of their inhospitality to foreigners and their downright hostility to the proselytizing efforts of the early Western missionaries. The Koreans have summed up their attitude in their saying: "The missionaries came to do good; they stayed and did well."

Ethiopia, a Coptic-Christian country, has by tradition an even greater antipathy to spreaders of the Christian gospel. European Christians are, by Monophysite standards, as much heretics as the followers of Islam. Indeed, until the beginning of the last century, Catholic priests venturing to preach in Ethiopia were killed on sight. The Protestant missionaries who came later to the East African high plateau did little to ingratiate themselves. The entire burden of their religious persuasion was an insult to the Ethiopians' cult of the Virgin and their veneration of the saints.

Yet it was these missionaries, and the commercial adventurers who followed them, who brought European language and the white man's culture to the people of Asia and Africa. As a result, the general attitude toward the West remains today an ambivalent one. In the twentieth century, leaders in both regions recognize the necessity for contact with European and American civilization and desire to participate in the world-wide technological advance that has taken place. They do not want to be left behind, at the same time that they do not want to relinquish their traditional ways. They desire the tools but resist the concomitant social revolution that would make the tools work. The old suspicions are difficult to eradicate. Although their earlier isolationist policy has been superseded by an anxious eagerness to catch up and communicate, there is always in the back of their minds the question, is this a new trick? Will European language only impose another, a more insidious kind of imperialism, over the mind? Is this why language teachers are imported so generously by the foreign aid programs of the so-called donor nations? Sophisticated Asians and Africans see the adoption of the foreign language of any great power as a menace to their national identities.

Although neither Korea nor Ethiopia was ever subjugated by European colonial masters, the annexation of Korea by Japan in 1910, was considered by Koreans to have been the result of their abandonment by the U.S.A. upon whom they depended for diplomatic intervention. Their liberation by the American occupation in 1945, after thirty-five years of anti-American indoctrination, was greeted by something less than the enthusiasm it deserved. Ethiopia, on the other hand, had its taste of colonialism in the six-year Italian occupation of 1935-1941.

It is against such a background of latent hostility and distrust, mixed with strong personal motivation for learning on the part of certain ambitious individuals, that the teacher of English in Asia or Africa must work. The psychology of the elite in emerging countries is complicated by various factors of history as well as of personal experience; the length and severity of previous European domination may serve to alienate the individual from Western culture, while a subconscious urge to associate himself with the prestige of the traditionally privileged group — by wearing its clothes or speaking its language — may prevail upon him to risk rejection by his less educated countrymen. In spite of his need for an LWC to participate in world affairs, there is the increasingly important pride in color which divides the Asian and African from the white West.

Whatever their attitude may be, however fragile their own national personality, the people of the developing countries of the world must face up to the necessity they have for communication beyond their own continental boundaries. To reach out effectively, they will need one of the European languages used in international relations. Recent studies of the role of second languages in developing areas, made by the Center for Applied Linguistics, Washington, D. C., lists three major needs for an LWC: (1) internal communication; (2) access to science and technology; and (3) external or international communication. The summary statement of the researchers indicates that, since most nations of Asia and Africa are multilingual, a common language for government administration, education, and trade within their borders is essential. Although Korean serves the first purpose mentioned above, it fails to satisfy the other two. Amharic, the official Ethiopic language, is deficient on all counts, as we shall see.

ENGLISH AS A SECOND LANGUAGE IN KOREA[13]

In Korea as in most of Asia, English is now mainly a language of wider communication in the sense of (2) and (3) above. However, in the period immediately following World War II, it had a much more important role to play internally. At the time of the American occupation, the official language of Korea was Japanese, and all positions of responsibility, including teaching posts, were held by Japanese. With the liberation, and the repatriation of the Japanese, the Korean language was reinstated and speaking Japanese became anathema to Koreans. It was soon apparent that the very existence of a national government, independent of interpreter control, was impossible without breaking down the language barrier which existed between the U. S. military and civilian officials (responsible for training the new government) and their Korean counterparts who were being trained. Korean, still classified as an "exotic language," was even more exotic in 1945 and was spoken by only a few American missionaries who had little preparation and less inclination to be involved in government administration. The educated Koreans, eligible for official positions had had at least several years of exposure to academic English — as it was then taught. Their achievement, in which they took considerable pride, consisted mainly in being able to translate Shakespeare with the aid of a bilingual (Japanese-English) dictionary.

Under the urgent demand for a crash English program, the American Language Institute was set up in Seoul early in 1946. It served to facilitate the civil affairs administration during the ensuing occupation period and also gave English language training to numerous Korean university students who had obtained scholarships to the U.S.A.

This good beginning was abruptly interrupted by the war of 1950 with its disruption of the school system and general disorganization of Korean society. Nearly two decades later, the country continues to rehabilitate itself under U.N. auspices. American military officers are still assigned tours of duty on the peninsula but now they arrive with full control of Korean, having undergone intensive training at the Defense Language Institute (formerly the Army Language School) in Monterey, California. There, taught by native speakers, they have had the advantage of the latest developments in second language instruction. Meanwhile, there is no longer the same urgent necessity for the Korean officials to master English and the American enthusiasm for sponsoring Korean students abroad has abated.

In present day Korea, where the activity of war has given away to the stalemate of Panmunjom, English has begun to return to its former place as a foreign language, but with a difference. Although it is now the second language of the country, replacing Japanese, English is not a public or official means of communication within Korea. It has rather a typical LWC role. Korean delegates to ASPAC in Seoul, or to the U.N. in New York, need to speak English. Students pursuing higher education in certain fields must have at least a reading knowledge of the language. As a result, when Korea returns to a normal peacetime state, English will undoubtedly be taught in the schools more extensively and more efficiently than before the war.

In other parts of Asia, the role of English varies with the country.[14] In the Philippines, for example, it is the common language, used from the third grade onward as the only medium of instruction in the schools. Here the function of English is obviously moving from that of a foreign language of the elite to a local language of the growing middle class. In Japan, on the other hand, the direction of development is reversed and more like that of Korea. After the artificially motivated period of the American occupation, the popular demand for spoken English has subsided at the same time that it is being taught more widely and efficiently in the schools as an LWC.[15] Although a large English Second Language program exists in mainland China, the widespread use of the language for purposes other than access to publications seems unlikely in the near future. What the role of English may be in Southeast Asia will depend on the outcome of the conflict there. On the basis of the experience with military occupation in Japan and Korea, we may expect a corresponding rise in the popular demand for spoken English (known in its Far-Eastern pidgin form as "Bamboo" English), depending on the extent of the penetration of American and Australian forces. In South Vietnam, for instance, English already supersedes French as the language of economic, political, and social preferment. In any event, we may anticipate that, for some time to come, English will be called on to offer a compromise solution to language diffculties in many of the developing areas of the world.

ENGLISH AS A SECOND LANGUAGE IN ETHIOPIA [16]

This trouble-shooting function of English is even more noticeable in Africa than in Asia. Indeed, the problem of language is probably more of an irritant to the smooth advancement of Sub-Sahara Africa than of any other region attempting a breakthrough into the twentieth century. It presents a constant barrier between educated peoples of different nations whose public language, usually a European tongue, may be French, Portugese, Italian, or English, according to the background of their country's colonial history.[17] It presents an obstacle to communication within the boundaries of a single territory, between tribes whose spoken tongues are various and often mutually unintelligible, so that the speakers, living in relative proximity, have little communication with each other and may even be hostile strangers.

With the founding of University College in Addis Ababa in 1950,[18] those Ethiopians who had aspirations for higher education found it imperative to acquire fluency in English, the language of instruction throughout the college. In the decade 1950-1960, various attempts were made to improve English instruction at the preparatory levels, but lack of funds for importing English speaking teachers from abroad, as well as for teacher training at home, continued to be an obstacle to significant improvement.

By 1961, when Haile Sellassie I University was inaugurated and American financial support was flowing into the country in more substantial amounts, greater official concern began to be given to the matter of second language learning at all levels. Numerous proposals were considered and several pilot projects were undertaken. One of them introduced Amharic as the language of instruction in the first six grades, with English taught only as a subject. In the seventh grade, and thereafter, according to this plan, *all* subjects would be taught in English as was formerly the practice for *most* subjects from the fourth grade. This experiment was an example of the growing awareness on the part of the government of the need to broaden the use of the national language in order to unify the country while, at the same time, retaining the English skills so necessary for communication with the rest of the world.

In any event, no matter what the scheme, certain difficulties remain. Only about one out of every five children of school age in Ethiopia has Amharic as a mother tongue. This means that a large majority of the children would have to acquire Amharic as a second language *at the same time* that instruction in all their subjects (except English — theoretically) is in Amharic. After six years of this taxing procedure, with English taught only as a subject, the pupils would have all their instruction in English, beginning with the seventh grade.

Obviously this puts a severely heavy burden on children already handicapped by inadequately trained teachers, insufficient or inappropriate textbooks, inadequate school facilities and a generally poor learning environment.

In the face of these seemingly insurmountable hazards, there are some Ethiopian educators who think that Amharic should be the language of instruction throughout the school system. They feel strongly that English should not be indefinitely the public language of their country. Pride in their own languages, [19] combined with a distaste for intellectual imperialism — which they see as a reliable concomitant of learning the language of any "advanced" nation — make them look forward with hope to that time when a revitalized Amharic may be able to cope with the needs of modern life at least within Ethiopia. They recognize that, as more Amharic-speaking teachers take the place of the "farengi" (expatriates) in the secondary school and university courses, it becomes palpably absurd for them to teach other Amharic-speaking students in English, a language which neither group fully understands. Meanwhile, the U.S. Peace Corps is working valiantly against frustrating odds to bring modern methods of language instruction to the schools.

In spite of these and many other problems, the future of English teaching in Ethiopia looks fairly bright. The Peace Corps has had its impact, while the increasing recognition of applied linguistics at the University, where Ethiopian linguists trained abroad are exerting a strong influence, promises to bring the language program into step with contemporary developments.

FOREGROUND — GENERAL EXPECTATIONS

The complexity of the language situation throughout Asia and Africa has been suggested in the brief account of the role of English in modern Korea and Ethiopia. Some attention has been given to the general language background of these areas in an effort to emphasize for the non-native teacher of a second language, the necessity for an understanding of the cultural matrix of which language in any society is a part.

Since knowledge of the cultural background of the people one expects to teach is such a necessary corollary of good performance, some notion of the linguistic diversity of the region involved, the use of its various indigenous languages and the prevalent attitude toward foreign languages, must be part of the equipment the expatriate teacher brings to a successful TESL strategy.

Concerning the role of English as a second language, it is possible to entertain certain expectations which have a high probability of fulfillment for any language teacher who may find himself in a developing country of Asia or Africa:

1) The general attitude toward English will vary according to the historical background of the country but usually it will be an ambivalent one.

2) In those countries with former colonial ties to Britain, English will be a prestige language and will be spoken well by the elite.

3) In Asia, English will be more often a second language, while in Africa it is more regularly a third (a. tribal tongue, b. official national language, c. European language as LWC).

4) Because of differences in opportunity for education, more men than women will speak English.

5) Urban populations will have more speakers of English than those of rural communities.

6) Metropolitan areas will usually have at least one English sound track movie theater, an English language radio station, an English newspaper, and one or more bookshops where English books and periodicals may be purchased.

7) English will be taught in the school system and may be the language of instruction at the upper educational levels, but a pervasive nationalizing trend favors the increasing use of a national language as the teaching medium.

8) Most of the younger educated citizens of the country will have some knowledge of English.

9) Motivation to learn English will be strong, especially among the young adult population. It will be stronger where there is an English-speaking community of potential employers.

10) Local TESL methodology will vary but will tend to be traditional, except in the regions served by a university or in metropolitan areas where English language influence

is strong and British Council, AID, or USIS English programs are organized. (The Commonwealth Conference on TESL, held at Makerere College, Kampala, Uganda, in January, 1961, has had a widespread effect on improving English language teaching throughout East Africa.)

11) The subject matter of the English course at the intermediate and advanced levels will normally be English literature. (The eighteenth and nineteenth century periods seem to be favored, with Goldsmith and Dickens taking the center of the stage in the high schools, while Browning and Hopkins are popular for detailed analysis in college classes.)

12) Little or no attention will be given to local literature in English, either Asian or African.

13) The majority of teachers of English in the primary grades will be nationals of the country, with less than twelve years of schooling. (They will have very little aural-oral control of English and must, therefore, rely on translation, dictation, or the explaining of English grammar in their mother tongue.)

14) The goal of language teaching will inevitably be the passing of written examinations which are, more often than not, geared to failure. (These examinations, set by a central authority, not only shape the course content but measure the competence of the teacher. Even the reputation of the individual school may be determined by the total number of "pass" marks in each case.)

15) Materials will be in short supply, usually outdated and culturally inappropriate, with anthologies of English literature predominating at the higher levels.

16) Facilities will be limited and unsuitable. (If there is a language laboratory, it will probably be unusable because of climate damage, equipment failure and/or the lack of technicians to repair it.)

17) Classes will not be homogeneous either in age or ability. Students will often be segregated by sex.

18) In Africa, the acquisition of English will usually suffer interference from at least two other languages.

19) The language course may be disrupted at any time by political interference. (A change in government could abruptly alter the LWC from English to Russian or even Chinese, without regard to linguistic disadvantages which might result for second language learners.)

20) Conditions under which language teaching is carried on will remain for some time volatile and unpredictable so that flexibility and imagination will continue to be two of the most important qualities an expatriate teacher can bring to her TESL assignment in the developing countries of Asia or Africa.

---

[1] Although Canada is officially a bilingual country, the new Canadian who settles outside Quebec needs only English for his vocational and social adjustment. Within Quebec, the majority of migrants, who are already French-speaking, generally find it advantageous to learn English as a second language.

[2] A pilot project of this kind has been organized in Montreal.

[3] Robert B. Kaplan, "Cultural Thought Patterns in Inter-Cultural Education," *Language Learning,* XVI, No. 1 & 2, (1966) pp. 1-21, reports on an analysis of some seven hundred foreign student compositions in English.

[4] *Ibid.,* p. 15.

[5] According to the Institute of International Education's *Open Doors,* of the total number of foreign students in U. S. universities, now approaching 100,000, the largest group comes from the Far East. The most popular major field of study is Engineering and the majority attend universities in California and New York. Approximately 10% of the total number is from Canada. These, together with about 2% from the U. K. and a small number from other English-speaking areas, generally have English as a mother tongue.

[6] See Margaret Gillett, "Orientation of Foreign Students in the U. S.," *Oversea Education,* January 1962.

[7] Columbia University Teachers College began in 1967 a new course, "Methods of Teaching Standard English as a Second Dialect." This course, designed for teachers of underprivileged children, is a specialized part of the "compensatory education" effort of the U. S. War on Poverty program.

[8] For a description of British programs, see Chap. V.

[9] For details about U. S. programs and degrees granted in the field, see the periodically revised publication, *University Resources in the United States for Linguistics and the Teaching of English as a Foreign Language,* published by the Center for Applied Linguistics, Washington, D. C.

[10] *A Survey of Twelve University Programs for the Preparation of TESOL,* (Washington, D. C.: Center for Applied Linguistics, 1966), p. 9.

[11] One of these, at Marianopolis College, Montreal, qualifies for credit for the B.A. in English with a concentration in Applied Linguistics.

[12] Under a suitably exotic title, "The Ozymandias Effect," Dr. Margaret Gillett of McGill University has explored a number of these difficulties in a paper she read at the Fourth Conference of the Canadian National Commission for UNESCO held in Montreal. This paper was subsequently published in *Dialogue 1965,* the National Conference Report, Canadian National Commission for UNESCO, Ottawa, p. 135-9.

[13] See M. Kehoe, "Teaching English in Korea," *Adult Education Journal*, January, 1949.

[14] No attempt has been made in this survey to touch on English in India or countries adjacent to it. The language problem on the entire subcontinent is so vast and confused that any effort to cover it would require far more space than could be given here. The Central Institute of English at Hyderabad is doing important research and experiments in TESL. Results of these are available in periodic reports.

[15] The influence of American applied linguistics is evident in many of the teaching materials recently published in Japan. Among the most noteworthy of these is the ELEC (English Language Education Council) Course in three volumes, designed for use in retraining programs for junior high school teachers of English. The texts are based on the oral approach of C. C. Fries who collaborated in their preparation.

[16] See M. Kehoe, "The Teaching of English as a Third Language in Ethiopia," *English Language Teaching*, April, 1964.

[17] For a discussion of Swahili and other African lingua francas, see W. J. Samarin, "Lingua Francas, with Special Reference to Africa," in Frank A. Rice, (ed.), *Study of the Role of Second Languages in Asia, Africa and Latin America* (Washington, D. C.: Center for Applied Linguistics, 1962).

[18] See M. Kehoe, "Higher Education in Ethopia," *Journal of Higher Education*, December, 1962.

[19] Besides Amharic, the main Ethiopic languages are Galla, Tigrinya, Sidamo, Tigre, and Gurage.

CONCLUSION

There is little doubt that technical advance, the increasing miniaturization of electronic devices, the proliferation of knowledge and its accelerated expansion will cause still further changes in the school and the curriculum. As decade follows decade into the twenty-first century, there will be so much to learn that educational planners will have to be constantly reassessing priorities. In the course of these revisions, and in view of the inevitable development of translation machines, the amount of time and money spent on acquiring foreign languages will certainly come under severe scrutiny. Ultimately the same question may be asked of foreign languages that has been asked of arithmetic. Should all pupils be required to learn those basic operations that machines can do better? Will foreign languages some day be considered such basic skills? Will the study of languages be finally relegated to a lower priority in the face of other more important kinds of knowledge? Or will the study of foreign languages be increased? How many foreign languages, if any, should a student be expected to learn? How early should he begin acquiring a second language? A third? If our methodology is streamlined, how many languages can a child learn at the same time? More and more such questions will be asked and more and more will be answered as applied linguistics extends its research.

SECOND LANGUAGE LEARNING AND A WORLD VIEW

Whatever the specific decisions taken about foreign languages, whether more are added to the curriculum or all are dropped, whether a second or third language is introduced early or late, simultaneously or sequentially, there is sure to be more emphasis in tomorrow's school on international understanding and appreciation of other cultures. Careful attention will be given to the choice of a second language, if any, on the basis of which one is likely to offer the maximum intercultural benefits. It is possible that by the year 2000 this might be, for Westerners, a non-European language, conceivably Chinese, Hindi or Arabic. One of the genuinely critical commentaries on our present education system in North America has been its provincialism. We have generally ignored Asia, Africa, and the Near East in our schools and colleges so that, in the past, our graduates have been able to earn degrees and terminate their formal education with no exposure whatever to non-European cultures. When they have had any introduction to the "mysterious East" or "darkest Africa," it has usually been just that — a prejudiced, partial, or stereotyped view.

Clearly this condition is already changing. Political and military involvement in the Far East, commitment to the U.N. responsibilities in Africa have forced us to take cognizance of the real world beyond our tight little Atlantic community. The introduction of Asia and Africa Studies, as well as courses in international and comparative education, has brought these no longer distant areas into our ken. As populations become more mobile, distances shrink and political boundaries continue to shift, we need greater rapport with people of different origins and backgrounds. How much of this rapport can be established through information brought to the student in his mother tongue, via comparative cultural studies, depends on the attention given the subject by educators. Certainly anyone can read the literatures of the world in translations which are probably better than those he could hope to make for himself and more meaningful than any appreciation he would have of the original work unless, of course, he is lucky enough to be a bicultural-bilingual in the languages concerned. Our academic need for a world view may, therefore, be best served for the time being, by a culturally oriented survey of world literatures (including Asian and African), backed up by courses in communication or language and culture, on the one hand, and related courses in comparative civilizations, their religious and ethical systems, on the other — *all given in the students' mother tongue.* The presently familiar liberal arts concentration on a single foreign language and literature (usually European) may be expected to give way to a broader cross-cultural, multi-disciplinary approach with much more recognition of non-Western contributions.

A CONTEMPORARY APPROACH
TO LANGUAGE TEACHING

As improved methods of language instruction begin to take effect, however, we may hope to see the student entering his thirteenth year of schooling in full command of at least one second language which will provide him with genuinely wider communication outside his own culture, be that Eastern or Western. His extended exposure to a world-wide network of communication media will have brought him information and stimulated his curiosity on many subjects not always adequately covered in his formal education — his horizons, as well as his vocabulary, will be expanded. Born under Telstar, he will bring to his studies a sharpened awareness. If he is not to find his formal education boring and unrelated to the life he lives outside the classroom, his teachers will have to devise new ways of handling subjects. Their job, from the beginning level to the most advanced, will be mainly one of motivation, innovation, and integration.

Although this may seem too neat, or too abstract, a summary of the teachers' role in the twenty-first century, it indicates the kind of flexible and imaginative approach more likely to supplement the programed materials that will be available to teachers everywhere. Immediately and more specifically, some of the steps that might be taken to update the teaching of languages, including the mother tongue, are these:

1) Give a better understanding of the nature and function of language itself, with more opportunity for the learners to use their language skills in meaningful (to them) situations.

2) Place more emphasis on the comprehension and manipulation of language for improving the understanding of other subjects in the schools.

3) Give some attention to the history of language and its relation to area studies.

4) Provide an exposure to language as an expression of the wider international culture.

5) Instill an awareness of the power of language to shape human behavior.

6) Speak the preferred speech of the area in which the teaching is done.

7) Put greater reliance on technological aids (such as educational broadcasting and televising, records and tapes) for assignments in critical listening, watching, and oral reporting.

This last point, "greater reliance on technological aids," deserves a closer look as the electronic laboratory becomes a common part of the equipment of the school.

AUTOMATED LANGUAGE LEARNING

It has been said that the invention of firearms gave the coup de grace to feudalism and initiated the industrial revolution. If so, then the parallel artifact of the airborne computerized gunner of the twentieth century may be said to have ushered in the electronic revolution of our own time. That the application of these forms of converted energy should have begun in power struggles is testimony, if need be, to the grand scale of our communication failure. The mechano-chemical robot of the future, with its synthetic polymers for muscle will, hopefully, have a chance to develop in a less hostile climate of interplanetary understanding. With the further improvements in communication systems presently forecast, the next techn logical revolution may not take even a generation to reach the common man.[1]

But education is slow in adjusting to widespread and cataclysmic social change. In its role as custodian of human culture, with its responsibility to shape the young in the image of the old, it tends to be suspicious of the new and to resist innovation. It distrusts the machine. Even when language departments install laboratories, teachers often show their resistance to change by failing to alter their approach to suit the new equipment. Then they complain because it doesn't bring the magical results advertized. The expensive gadgetry is there but the goal is not achieved. This is unfortunate since language learning is by its very nature one of the most appropriate kinds of activity for automated instruction.

Nevertheless, in spite of opposition and delay, acceptance is bound to come. Economic considerations, which more and more dominate and shape the educational scene, will finally force the issue where philosophic reasons have failed. As the automated classroom, with its mass-produced learning machines, proves to be the cheapest way of coping with the education explosion, so the ideal of individualized instruction will inadvertently be realized, with each student facing his own program and advancing at his own speed. Alteration in methodology will follow, in due course, as the teacher's rejection is overcome and he learns to cooperate with the machine that can relieve him of so much of his burden of nonteaching duties. He will begin to appreciate that technological aids do not threaten him. They can be made to serve his needs instead. Relieved of drill work and the disciplinary problems of a large inactive and often inattentive class, he will have more time in the lab to function directly with the individual student in a more personal relationship. With better materials, provided by the specialized programming staff of a central language development center, he will be encouraged to try the techniques of modern methodology. Released from the deadly job of correcting badly written themes on trivial subjects, he will have time after school to undertake the retraining course that will improve his competence and increase his professional status.

Such a course will be necessary, periodically, just to keep up with changes resulting from research in applied linguistics and communication technology. Many of those now in high school, who may be planning on teaching as a career, will find themselves working as programmers instead. Much of the leadership in tomorrow's education will be in the hands of those who create the programs for the machines. Recent developments in language lab equipment,[2] involving computer processing of speech signals and evaluation of student responses, suggest the rapidly increasing sophistication of this type of educational hardware. The potential capability of language learning machines can scarcely be imagined as we step on the launching pad of the twenty-first century.

LANGUAGE AND THE COMPUTER: MACHINE TRANSLATION

The alliance between linguistics and the machine takes on its most exciting possibilities with translation by computer.

"But processing natural language on a computer calls for precise, accurate, voluminous knowledge of the linguistic behavior of the speakers or authors whose utterances or writings are to be processed."[3] In fact, it may call for a great deal more. Machine to machine communication across cultures, via some still undeveloped third computer language, boggles the imagination of even the most ardent disciple of "one world."

Yet people have puzzled over the fascinating question of an international language for a long time. More than seven hundred attempts have been made, from Bacon's day to ours, to invent an auxiliary universal language. Of these, Esperanto, alone with its Latin-style grammar and European vocabulary, has caught on — and that only in a limited way. Computer languages, algebraically oriented as they are, offer at present slightly better prospect of success as a medium of universal communication. Their contribution to international exchange of ideas is more likely to be through "instantaneous" translation of natural languages, a process still beset by enormous difficulties. But our age is an age of faith — faith in science — and science stands to be among the first beneficiaries of automated translation.

In machine language "the total repertoire of admissible instructions forms a finite, precise vocabulary which may be considered as a particular computer language in terms of which the programer can communicate with the machine."[4] The computer language is, therefore, individual to the machine using it. The most widely known at present are IBM's *FORTRAN* (formula translating system),[5] an algebraic language of some complexity, *ALGOL,* a problem-oriented language, developed in Europe, *MAD,* (Michigan Algorithm Decoder), *PL/I,* a post-*Fortran* programming language, and *COBOL* (Common Business-Oriented Language), designed for nontechnical applications. All of these are based on the same logic-flow diagram and are not difficult to read, once the machine vocabulary has been mastered. "But the advantage of a sound working knowledge of *Fortran* goes beyond such generalities, since . . . a programer who knows *any* computer language *well* will have little difficulty learning another one when the need arises."[6] Unfortunately computers manufactured by different firms use different languages, and the machines of a few years ago are beginning to be obsolescent, unable to take the newer, more elaborate codes. To bridge these gaps, a program must be devised to translate one computer language into another. When this is done, we shall begin to have something approximating a universal machine code.

Meanwhile, important research in problems of MT (machine translation) proceeds at university and industrial centers,[7] From the point of view of the linguist, language-data processing "includes such fields as machine translation, information storage and retrieval (if based on natural language), automatic abstracting, certain intelligence applications, and the like. All these activities can be summed up under the heading of *linguistic information processing*."[8] The translation machine, in order to fulfill its capabilities, will need to recognize both the phonetic and graphic sign components of language.[9] The former poses an additional problem of context searching routine to establish which of several words that sound alike is intended in any particular position. Since recognition of the graphic sign component presents fewer problems, the evolution of machine translation of written texts has preceded that of spoken language. If automated dictionaries and libraries are feasible, the linguistic problems of analysis and synthesis, in terms of morphology, lexicography, syntax and semantics, can also be solved. Even at the present, relatively clumsy, beginning stage, Russian-English translation "is done at the rate of 45,000 words per hour, or 750 words per minute, or 12.5 words per second."[10]

But the translation machine will not put the foreign language teacher on the shelf, anymore than the teaching machine has replaced the teacher. It is unfortunate, and a profound mistake on the part of those who first marketed machines for the classroom, that they did not bill them for what they are, mechanical *learning* devices. Much of the resistance to them could have been eliminated. Indeed, the entire field of education could improve its image if the emphasis were shifted from teaching to learning. Within the scope of our immediate interest, LESL will receive increasing attention in Applied Linguistics, rather than TESL.

Even though the word, "teaching," inevitably creeps into the text, the teachers who have contributed to this book have been constantly aware of the role of the teacher as a *guide* to the learner and the function of teaching as an *aid* to learning. Technological developments can only professionalize and diversify the work of the teacher while they facilitate the task of the learner, whether he is at arm's length in the classroom or at airwave length a hemisphere away.

M. K.

---

[1] For introductory reading on man and the machine, see Neville Moray, *Cybernetics* (New York: Hawthorne Books, 1963).

[2] See H. Lane and R. Buiten, "Self-Instructional Device for Conditioning Accurate Prosody," in A. Valdman, *Trends in Language Teaching* (New York: McGraw-Hill, 1966), pp. 159-175.

[3] David G. Hays, "Research Procedures in Machine Translation," in Paul L. Garvin (ed.), *Natural Language and the Computer* (New York: McGraw-Hill, 1963), p. 183.

[4] Michel A. Melkanoff, "Computer Languages," in Garvin, *op.cit.,* p. 84.

[5] There are, to date, several *Fortrans*, I, II, III, and IV, to correspond with the computers they serve.

[6] C. M. Thatcher and A. J. Capato, *Digital Computer Programming: Logic and Language* (Reading, Mass.: Addison-Wesley Publishing Co.), p. 137.

[7] Such as the Massachusetts Institute of Technology, the University of California at Los Angeles; Bunker-Ramo Corp. and Ramo Woolridge, Inc. at Canoga Park; and the Rand Corp. in Santa Monica.

[8] Paul L. Garvin, "A Linguist's View of Language-data Processing," in Garvin (ed.), *op.cit.,* p. 109.

[9] For a good summary treatment of MT and the computer, see the paper by Halliday, "Linguistics and Machine Translation," in Angus McIntosh and M. A. K. Halliday, *Patterns of Language* (London, Longmans, Green & Co. Ltd., 1966), pp. 145-158.

[10] Jules Mersel, "Programming Aspects of Machine Translation," in Garvin (ed.), *op. cit.,* p. 251.

APPENDIX I

Speech Organs [1]

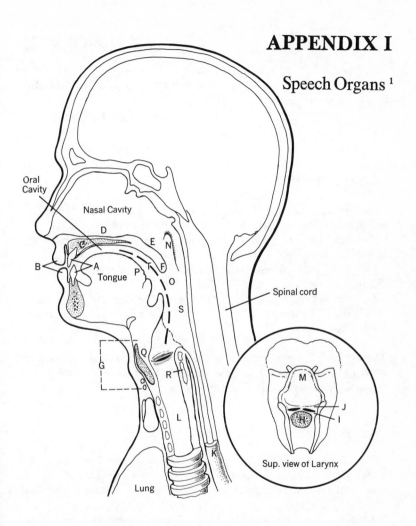

A Teeth	K Esophagus
B Lips	L Trachea
C Alveolar Ridge	M Epiglottis
D Hard Palate	N Nasopharynx
E Soft Palate (Velum)	O Oropharynx
F Uvula	P Dorsum
G Larynx	Q Thyroid Cartilage
H Glottis	R Cricoid Cartridge
I Vocal Cord (True)	S Pharyngeal Cavity
J Vocal Cord (False)	T Vocal Tract

APPENDIX II

Selected Publications
and Materials

BIBLIOGRAPHIES

Comité International Permanent de Linguistes. *Bibliographie Linguistique de l'Année.* Utrecht: Spectrum, 1949-. 1 vol. per year.

Nostrand, Howard L., David W. Foster and Clay B. Christensen. *Research on Language Teaching: An Annotated International Bibliography,* 1945-1964. 2d ed. Seattle: University of Washington Press, 1965, 373 pp.

Ohannessian, Sirarpi (ed.). *Reference List of Materials for English as a Second Language.* Washington: Center for Applied Linguistics, 1964-1966, 2 vols.

The above bibliographies may be supplemented, for the period since 1966, by announcements of new books and periodicals which appear regularly in the Linguistic Reporter.

GENERAL

The Bobbs-Merrill Reprint Series in Language and Linguistics. The Bobbs-Merrill Co., Inc., 4300 West 62 St., Indianapolis, Ind., U.S.A. Loose-leaf reprints of articles which have become classics in the field. Write for listing.

Language and Language Learning. Oxford University Press, Amen House, London E. C. 4. A series of writings from linguistics, language study, language teaching methodology and materials. Write for their list.

Longman's Linguistic Library. Longmans Green and Co., Ltd., 48 Grovesnor St., London W. 1. A series of books for specialists in the fields of education and teaching of languages.

Monograph Series on Languages and Linguistics. Institute of Language and Linguistics, Georgetown University, Washington, D. C. Annual reports with one section on teaching language skills.

Occasional Papers. American Language Institute of New York University, Washington Square, N. Y. C., N. Y. Order from Educational Division, Chilton Books, 401 Walnut St., Philadelphia, Penn. 19106. Biannual publication with TEFL discussions and book reviews.

30 Books for TEFL. Center for Applied Linguistics, 1717 Massachusetts Ave. N.W., Washington, D.C. 20036. A twelve page annotated list of background readings, books on methodology and textbooks.

TEN BOOKS SELECTED IN ORDER OF DIFFICULTY[1]

1 Stevrick, Earl W. *Helping People Learn English—A Manual for Teachers of English as a Second Language.* New York, Nashville: Abingdon Press, 1957. 138 pp. This compact book discusses concepts of language, language learning, language teaching, the sounds of English, and English grammar.

2 Dacanay, Fe. R. *Techniques and Procedures in Second Language Teaching.* PCLS Monograph Series 3. Quezon City: Phoenix Publishing House, 1963. 538 pp. This monograph give practical applications of linguistics to language teaching. Topics include presentation of English structure, pattern practice, reading, writing, spelling, and testing with techniques and procedures illustrated. The above two books are highly recommended for the teacher inexperienced in TESL.

3 Stevick, Earl W. *A Workbook in Language Teaching.* Nashville: Abingdon Press, 1963. 127 pp. A companion volume to *Helping People Learn English,* this book demands "active responses" from the reader which develops language teaching skills.

4 Billows, F. L. *The Techniques of Language Teaching.* London: Longmans, Green, 1961. 259 pp. This book is directed towards the teaching of all foreign languages. It emphasizes the situational approach to language teaching.

5 Gauntlett, J. O. *Teaching English as a Foreign Language.* Rev. ed. London: Macmillan, 1961. 128 pp. Like Billows, Gauntlett is British. These two books should acquaint the teacher with British thinking on second-language teaching. Gauntlett's book is designed for the teaching of English to more or less advanced students.

6 Fries, Charles C. *Teaching and Learning English as a Foreign Language.* Ann Arbor: University of Michigan Press, 1945. 153pp. This work is a classic in the field. It discusses the "oral approach" and such impor-

---

[1]This list was compiled by Dr. E. Calimag.

tant topics as contextual orientation (culture in language teaching), mastering of sounds, structure, and vocabulary.

7 Politzer, Robert L. *Foreign Language Learning: A Linguistic Introduction*. Englewood Cliffs: Prentice-Hall, 1965. 155 pp. This book stresses the learning aspect of primarily four languages—English, French, Spanish, and German, as well as foreign language learning problems in general.

8 Brooks, Nelson. *Language and Language Learning: Theory and Practice*. New York, Burlingame: Harcourt, Brace, 1964. 238 pp. This volume presents a comprehensive discussion of language and language learning and teaching theory and methods.

9 Allen, Harold B. (ed.). *Teaching English as a Second Language: A Book of Readings*. New York: McGraw-Hill, 1965. 406 pp. This volume contains articles by forty-five contributing authors from varied backgrounds—British, America, Australian, Canadian and Philippine.

10 Lado, Robert. *Language Teaching: A Scientific Approach*. New York: McGraw-Hill, 1964. 239 pp. It is recommended that this book be read after the first seven books in this list. Lado, like Fries, is a well-known scholar on TEFL. His book is divided into three parts—language and language learning, language teaching, and technical aids.

JOURNALS

Bulletin on International Education. American Council on Education, 1785 Massachusetts Ave. N.W. Washington, D. C. 20036.

College English. National Council of Teachers of English, 508 South Sixth Street, Champaign, Ill., U.S.A.

Communications. Canadian Service for Overseas Students and Trainees, 338 Somerset St. West, Ottawa, Ontario, Canada.

English — A New Language. Commonwealth Office of Education, N. Sydney, N.S.W. Australia. For teachers of English to new Australians.

English Language Teaching. c/o W. R. Lee, Editor, 16 Alexandria Gardens, Hounslow, Middlesex, England.

Foreign Language Annals. Modern Language Association of America, 4 Washington Place, New York, N.Y. 10003.

Glottodidactica. Institute of Applied Linguistics, ul. Matejki 48/49, Poznan, Poland. An international journal with articles in French, English, German and Russian.

Hispania. American Association of Teachers of Spanish and Portuguese, University of Massachusetts, Amherst, Mass. 01002, U.S.A.

Language Learning. English Language Institute, University of Michigan, Ann Arbor, Michigan, U.S.A.

Linguistic Reporter. Center for Applied Linguistics, 1755 Massachusetts Ave. N.W., Washington, D. C. 20036.

N.E.A. Journal. National Education Association of U. S., 1201 16th St. N.W., Washington, D. C. 20036. Occasional articles on TESL.

Periodicals of Interest to TESOL. Center for Applied Linguistics, Washington, D. C. Annotated list of 22 periodicals.

Research in Education. Superintendent of Documents, U. S. Government Printing Office, Washington, D. C. 20402. Published by the U.S. Office of Education.

T. A. Informations. André Deweze, editor, 19 quai de la Graille, 38 Grenoble, France. Published by the Association pour la Traduction Automatique et de la Linguistique Appliquée (ATALA). International review of the application of computers to language analysis, in French or English.

TEFL. c/o TEFL, Center of English Language Research and Teaching, American University of Beirut, Beirut, Lebanon. A bulletin for the teaching of English as a foreign language.

Word. Secretary-Treasurer, Linguistic Circle of New York, Inc. c/o Compton 102, The City College, New York, N.Y. 10031.

APPENDIX III

Information Sources

The following is a selected list arranged in alphabetical order of organizations to which you may write for information. There is an emphasis on sources which offer further language training and provide information on teaching opportunities.

Advancement and Placement Institute. 167 N. 9 St., Brooklyn, N.Y., N. Y. Publishes "Crusade" which contains announcements of TESL jobs abroad.

American Council of Learned Societies. 345 E. 46 St., N. Y., N. Y. 10017. Offers grants for postgraduate summer study in linguistics.

American Council on Education. 1785 Massachusetts Ave. N.W., Washington, D. C. 20036. Exchange professorships abroad.

Anglo-Continental School of English. 29-35 Winsborne Road, Bournemouth, England. Private institution which teaches English to adult foreign students in mainly Europe.

The Applied Linguistics Foundation (TALF). The Hague-West, The Netherlands. An organization serving the Benelux countries and operating Practical Summer Schools of Linguistics in various areas.

Association of Commonwealth Universities. Marlborough House, Pall Mall, London S. W. 1, England. For university level posts in ESL.

Association of Universities and Colleges of Canada. 151 Slater Street, Ottawa 4, Canada. Booklet on admission requirements of Canadian universities.

L'Asociacion Chilena de Profesores e Investigadores de la Lengua y Literatura (APIL). c/o Dr. Rudolf Oroz, APIL, Chile Information about language studies in Latin America.

L'Association Internationale de Linguistique Appliquée (AILA). c/o Assoc. Française de la Linguistique Appliquée, 9 rue Lhomond, Paris 5e, France. Organizes international colloquia in the field.

Bell School of Languages. School of English for Foreign students, Red Cross Lane, Cambridge, England. Private institution.

Berlitz Schools. There are more than 300 located throughout the world. For positions in Europe and Africa: L'Association Internationale des Ecoles Berlitz, 31 Blvd. des Italiens, Paris 2e, France. For positions in

Asia: Berlitz School, 2 Kowa Bld., 11-39, 1-chome Akasaka, Minato-ku, Tokyo, Japan. For North America: 855 Third Avenue, New York, N. Y. 10022; 1 Place Ville Marie, Montreal, Quebec.

Bureau of Indian Affairs. Education Section, U. S. Department of Interior, Washington, D. C. 20242. In service training for teachers of non-English speaking American Indians.

The British Association for Applied Linguistics (BAAL). c/o Mr. D.A. Wilkins, Dept. of Linguistic Science, University of Reading, Reading, England.

British Council. Appointments Branch, 65 Davies St., London, W. 1., England. Handles appointments in schools and universities in all parts of the world. Local offices in most major cities. Publishes "British Council Staff Recruitment."

British Teachers Overseas Association. 77 Wembly Park, Wembly, Middlesex, England. Summer tour vacancies for teachers.

Bureau pour l'Enseignement de la Langue et de la Civilization Française à l'Etranger (BELC). 9 rue Lhomond, Paris 5e, France.

Canadian Department of Northern Affairs and National Resources. 410 Kent-Alberta Blvd., Ottawa 4, Ontario. For teaching in Eskimo and Indian schools.

Canadian Government Travel Bureau. 150 Kent St., Ottawa 4, Ontario. Published booklet, "Summer Courses in Canada, 1967."

Canadian Service for Overseas Students and Trainees (CSOST). 338 Somerset Street West, Ottawa, Ontario. Publishes newsletter, "Communications."

Canadian Summer School of Linguistics. Write to the University of Alberta and/or the Canadian Linguistics Association. This is held in Edmonton, Alberta and includes courses in TESL methods.

Canadian University Services Overseas (CUSO). Ottawa, Ontario. Like the U. S. Peace Corps, sends young people abroad to participate in educational and social development.

Catholic Overseas Appointments. Hinsley House, 38 King Street, London W. C. 2, England. Recruits for teachers in Catholic schools abroad.

Center for Applied Linguistics. 1717 Massachusetts Ave. N. W., Washington D. C. 20036. Clearing house for all TESL/TEFL information. Its newsletter is *Linguistic Reporter.*

Center for English Language Research and Teaching. American University of Beirut, Beirut, Lebanon.

Centre for Information in Language Teaching (CILT). State House, High Holborn, London W. C. 1, England. Clearing house, references library, documentation service, registry for TESL in Britain.

Centro de Linguistica Aplicada Instituto de Idiomas Yazigi. Rua Aurora, 713, São Paulo, Brazil. Linguistic orientation and research, teaching material and pedagogical planning, and teacher training.

College Entrance Examination Board. 475 Riverside Drive, N. Y., N. Y. 10027. Publishes "Handbook on Summer Institutes, 1965" and "Speaking About Teaching." Also administers tests used by many universities for entrance requirements.

Committee on International Exchange of Persons. 2101 Constitution Ave. N.W., Washington, D. C. 20418. Administers Fulbright Lectureships in Linguistics and TESL/TEFL.

Commonwealth Office of Education. North Sydney, N.S.W. Australia. Information on Colombo Plan and other government aid programs, migrant education, TESL research.

Company of Young Canadians. Box 1520 Ottawa, Ontario. Volunteer, domestic, social service program organized by the Canadian Government for work in depressed areas.

Council on Student Travel (CST). 777 United Nations Plaza, N. Y., N. Y. 10017. Federation of academic institutions, educational and religious organizations, sponsors tours abroad. Shipboard ESL programs for foreign students.

Defense Language Institute (DLI). English Language School, Lockland Air Force Base, Texas. English courses for foreign military students of all services. Headquarters of the Defense Language Institute, U. S. Naval Station, Anacostia Annex, Washington, D. C. 82536.

English Language Institute. University of Hawaii, Honolulu, Hawaii.

English Language Institute. University of Michigan, 2001 North University Building, Ann Arbor, Michigan.

English Language Services, Inc. 1620 Belmont St. N. W., Washington, D. C. 20009.

English Teaching Information Centre (ETIC). State House, 63 High Holborn, London W. C. 1, England. English teaching overseas.

Eurocentre. 36 Honor Oak Road, London, S. E. 23, England. Private organization operating several centers in the London area offering TEFL and area studies.

European Council of International Schools. Box 66, Kilchberg-Zurich, Switzerland.

Experiment in International Living. Putney, Vermont 05346, U. S. A. TEFL programs in many foreign countries.

Ford Foundation. 477 Madison Avenue, N. Y., N. Y. 10022. International training and research.

Fulbright Lectureships. See Committee on International Exchange of Persons.

Gabbitas-Thring Services, Ltd. 6 Sackville St., London 1, England. Private agency, no fees.

Institute of International Education. 809 United Nations Plaza, N.Y., N. Y. 10017.

Institute of Languages and Linguistics. Georgetown University, Washington, D. C. 20007.

International Student Information Service. 133 rue Hôtel des Monnaies, Brussels 6, Belgium. Publishes "Jobs Abroad."

Inter-University Council. 33 Bedford Place, London W. C. 1, England. For university appointments overseas.

Language Programs for the Disadvantaged. Center for Applied Linguistics, Washington, D. C. A report of a special committee of the National Council of Teachers, 1965.

Ministry of Overseas Development. Commonwealth Relations Office, Room 404, Eland House, Stag Place, London S. W. 1, England.

National Association for Foreign Student Affairs (NAFSA). 809 United Nations Plaza, New York, N. Y. 10017.

National Council of Teachers of English. 508 South Sixth Street, Champaign, Ill., U. S. A.

Near East College Association. Inter-Church Bldg., Riverside Dr., N. Y., N. Y. 10027. Processes applications for a number of schools and colleges in the Middle East, including Robert College, Istanbul, and the American University, Beirut, Lebanon.

Nuffield Foreign Languages Teaching Materials Project. c/o Phonetic Department, the University of Leeds, Leeds 2, England.

Peace Corps. 806 Connecticut Ave. N. W., Washington, D. C. 20525. Offers opportunities for overseas service to U.S. teachers, *et al.*

Pitman School of English. 46 Goodge Street, London W. 1., England. A private school specializing in teaching EFL.

The Planning Centre for the Teaching of English. Terra Sancta College, Jerusalem, Israel. Publishes "English Teaching Bulletin."

Royal Commission on Bilingualism and Biculturalism. P. O. Box 1508, Ottawa, Ontario, Canada.

Swan School of English. 117 Banbury Road, Oxford, England. Private institution offering programs in EFL.

TESL Materials Development Center. Teachers College, Columbia University, N. Y., N. Y. 10027. TESL materials for elementary schools.

TESOL—Teachers of English to Speakers of Other Languages. A professional association for those concerned with TESL/TEFL.

Times Educational Supplement. Printing House Square, London, E. C. 4 or 56 Hanover Street, Edinburgh 2, Scotland. Weekly classified advertisements for all types of TESL/TEFL positions. Probably the best source of such announcements.

UNESCO (United Nations Educational, Scientific and Cultural Organization). Place de Fontenoy, Paris 7e, France. Publishes "Study Abroad" which lists almost 2,000 opportunities for overseas study in all fields. Also, "Teaching Abroad" which lists opportunities for teaching overseas. Available at libraries, booksellers or government printers. Write for their publications list.

USAID (United States Agency for International Development). Education Service, U. S. Department of State, Washington, D. C. 20523. Supports TESL activities in thirty developing countries.

USIA (United States Information Agency). English Teaching Division, 1711 New York Ave. N.W., Washington, D. C. 20547. Conducts English teaching programs in more than fifty-five countries. Broadcasts English lessons over the Voice of America network in many countries.

U. S. Office of Education. Department of Health, Education, Welfare. Offers grants for TESOL summer institutes under the National Defense Education Act (NDEA). Also write to: Modern Foreign Language Institutes Section, Division of Educational Personnel Training, Bureau of Elementary and Secondary Education.